OXFORD
UNIVERSITY PRESS

Janet Hardy-Gould

English Plus

Workbook 1

OXFORD
UNIVERSITY PRESS

Great Clarendon Street, Oxford OX2 6DP

Oxford University Press is a department of the University of Oxford.
It furthers the University's objective of excellence in research, scholarship,
and education by publishing worldwide in

Oxford New York

Auckland Cape Town Dar es Salaam Hong Kong Karachi
Kuala Lumpur Madrid Melbourne Mexico City Nairobi
New Delhi Shanghai Taipei Toronto

With offices in

Argentina Austria Brazil Chile Czech Republic France Greece
Guatemala Hungary Italy Japan Poland Portugal Singapore
South Korea Switzerland Thailand Turkey Ukraine Vietnam

OXFORD and OXFORD ENGLISH are registered trade marks of
Oxford University Press in the UK and in certain other countries

ISBN: 978 0 19 474860 5   Workbook
ISBN: 978 0 19 474884 1   MultiROM
ISBN: 978 0 19 474876 6   Pack

Printed in China

This book is printed on paper from certified and well-managed sources.

ACKNOWLEDGEMENTS

Illustrations by: Paul Daviz p.6, 41; David Oakley p.66, 68; Gregory Roberts p.4,
9, 48; Stephanie Strickland/Poggio p.8, 11, 16, 18, 33, 40, 42, 59, 64.

Cover photographs: Getty (students/Ken Kaminesky), iStockphoto (Hikers/Sergiy
Zavgorodny), (Friends taking photo/Damir Cudic); PunchStock (Teen girls
listening to music/Photodisc).

*The publisher would like to thank the following for their permission to reproduce
photographs:* Alamy Images pp.8 (girl/Mikael Bertmar), 21 (Tyne Bridge,
Newcastle/nagelestock.com), 23 (Bristol Cathedral/Greg Balfour Evans),
39 (Sumatran Tiger/Arco Images GmbH), 44 (Summerhill school/Piers
Cavendish/Imagestate Media Partners Limited - Impact Photos), 51 (Astronaut
Neil Armstrong/Art Directors & TRIP), 67 (Jorge Posada of the New York
Yankees/Roger Kirkpatrick/VWPics/Visual&Written SL); Allstar Picture Library
p.58 (Nicole Kidman/Graham Whitby Boot); Arnos Design Ltd pp.7 (school
bags), 7 (DVDs), 95 (Moroccan flag/), 95 (Italian flag), 95 (Spanish flag), 95 (US
flag), 95 (Australian flag), 95 (Canadian flag), 95 (UK flag), 95 (Chinese flag);
Corbis pp.37 (elephant keeper/Bernd Vogel/Cusp), 51 (Christopher Columbus/
Leonardo de Selva), 51 (Pele/Hulton-Deutsch Collection), 51 (Queen Victoria/
Bettmann), 51 (Guglielmo Marconi/Bettmann); Dreamstime pp.5 (pen/Kiril
Roslyakov), 12 (girls with dog/David Davis), 32 (parrot/Ken Toh), 32 (seal/
Tom Dowd), 32 (chameleon/Outdoorsman), 32 (frog/Janpietruszka), 69 (York
Minster/Dale Mitchell); FLPA p.34 (falcon attacking starlings/Michael Durham);
Getty Images pp.10 (Footballer Wayne Rooney/Man Utd via Getty Images Chris
Bernard), 25 (Moroccan boy/Abdelhak Senna/AFP), 51 (Bust of Julius Caesar/
FPG), 52 (Marie Curie/Agence France Presse/Hulton Archive), 55 (Birmingham,
England/Travel Ink/Gallo Images), 59 (Wayne Rooney/Gallo Images), 60 (boy
with Rubik's Cube/Mark Sullivan); iStockphoto pp.7 (dog/Todd McLean),
7 (whiteboard/Carlos Alvarez), 12 (girl listening to music/Eliza Snow),
28 (Montreal/Victor Kapas), 32 (blue fly/arlindo71), 32 (snake/Lara Seregni),
32 (spider/Barbara Henry), 32 (shark/Chuck Babbitt), 34 (black bear/Keith
Binns), 36 (bee hive/Geoff Kuchera), 56 (tennis player/Marilyn Nieves),
56 (female tennis player/Chris Bernard); Oxford University Press pp.5 (teen
boy/Blend Images), 5 (teen girl/Blend Images), 5 (girl/Thinkstock), 5 (man/
Image Source), 10 (Boy outdoors/Haddon Davies), 10 (teenage girl/Imageshop),
12 (Boy mountain biking/Thinkstock), 15 (Girl using mobile phone/Radius
Images), 24 (Asian teen boy/Photodisc), 25 (Girl smiling/Photodisc), 25 (Boy
with rucksack/Ingram), 26 (Boy waking up/Corbis), 26 (Businesswoman
checking watch/MIXA), 26 (Girls at cafe/Photodisc), 26 (Man eating pizza and
watching tv/Pixland), 26 (Teenage girl doing homework/Purestock), 26 (Boy
sleeping/Photodisc), 32 (owl/Ingram), 32 (bear/Photodisc), 56 (Marathon runners
/Lew Beach), 56 (High jump/David Madison/Photographer's Choice), 56 (Football
/Moodboard), 56 (Race/Creatas), 95 (Brazilian flag/Graphi-Ogre), 95 (Japanese
flag/Photodisc); Photolibrary pp.34 (seal/Doug Allan/OSF), 34 (baby caiman in
mothers mouth/Mark MacEwen/OSF), 71 (rock climbing/White); Press Association
Images p.62 (Tanni Grey-Thompson/Gareth Copley); PunchStock p.58 (girl
with glasses/Image Source); Rex Features pp.13 (Orlando Bloom), 24 (Claudia
Schiffer/David Fisher), 57 (Rafael Nadal/Nils Jorgensen), 63 (Lewis Hamilton);
Robert Harding World Imagery p.20 (Sark/Geoff Renner); Science Photo Library
p.50 (Villa Griffone/Sheila Terry); Shutterstock pp.7 (boy by door/Sonya
Etchison), 7 (laptop/jossnat), 34 (spider/LionH), 65 (elephant/Paul Prescott); The
National Trust Photo Library p.53 (Chedworth Roman villa/Ian Shaw).

Contents

VOCABULARY ▪ A classroom

1 ⭐ Find thirteen more words.

D	I	C	T	I	O	N	A	R	Y	F	W
E	C	L	O	C	K	Z	V	U	S	G	I
S	W	Q	L	V	S	H	E	L	F	C	N
K	R	Z	A	W	L	J	M	E	Y	D	D
U	H	B	P	O	S	T	E	R	T	P	O
B	D	G	T	Z	V	I	M	Q	C	L	W
A	D	B	O	A	R	D	S	K	H	A	N
G	F	M	P	N	D	O	O	R	A	Y	U
P	J	C	S	F	S	K	H	V	I	E	L
N	O	T	E	B	O	O	K	Z	R	R	Z

__dictionary__

1 _____   8 _____
2 _____   9 _____
3 _____   10 _____
4 _____   11 _____
5 _____   12 _____
6 _____   13 _____
7 _____

2 ⭐⭐ Look at the pictures and complete the sentences with words in exercise 1.

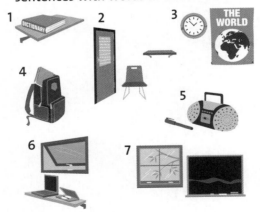

1 The __dictionary__ is on the shelf.
2 The _____ is between the shelf and the door.
3 The _____ is next to the poster.
4 The _____ is in the bag.
5 The _____ is next to the pen.
6 The _____ and the DVD are under the window.
7 The board is near the _____.

3 ⭐⭐ Look at the picture and complete the sentences with the correct prepositions.

The door is _____near_____ the board.

1 The clock is _____ the window and the door.
2 The bag is _____ the chair.
3 The chair is _____ the door.
4 The ruler is _____ the bag.
5 The CD player is _____ the shelf.
6 The CD player is _____ the board.

4 ⭐⭐⭐ Complete the lists with words in exercise 1.

Things in my bag.	Things in my bedroom.
_____pen_____	_____shelf_____
_____	_____
_____	_____
_____	_____
_____	_____
_____	_____
_____	_____

LANGUAGE FOCUS ■ Possessive 's and subject and object pronouns • Possessive adjectives

Possessive 's

1 ⭐⭐ **Follow the lines. Then write the names with the possessive 's and the objects.**

Sara —————— bags
1 the teacher ————— dictionary
2 the girl ————— pen
3 Tom ————— teacher
4 the boys ————— CD player
5 the teachers ————— poster
6 the students ————— DVDs

Sara's CD player. _____

1 _____
2 _____
3 _____
4 _____
5 _____
6 _____

Subject pronouns and possessive adjectives

2 ⭐ **Complete the table with the words in the box.**

> Your   We   His   + My   They   You
> Its   She

Subject pronoun	Possessive adjective
¹ *I* 'm twelve years old.	² _____ pen.
³ _____ 're from France.	Your desk.
He's a student.	⁴ _____ notebook.
⁵ _____ 's from England.	Her dictionary.
It's a good DVD.	⁶ _____ name.
⁷ _____ 're eleven years old.	Our laptop.
You're a teacher.	⁸ _____ board.
⁹ _____ 're from the USA.	Their poster.

3 ⭐⭐ **Complete the sentences.**

A   Use possessive adjectives.

you / DVD   It's _your_ DVD.

1 he / laptop   It's _____ laptop.
2 we / classroom   It's _____ classroom.
3 I / dictionary   It's _____ dictionary.
4 she / bag   It's _____ bag.
5 the teachers /   It's _____ CD player.
  CD player

B   Use subject pronouns.

the girl / in my class

  She 's in my class.

6 Carlos and Marina / our teachers
   _____ 're our teachers.
7 Mia and I / in class 1B
   _____ 're in class 1B.
8 the laptop / on the desk
   _____ 's on the desk.
9 the dictionaries / on the shelf
   _____ 're on the shelf.
10 David / twelve years old
   _____ 's twelve years old.

4 ⭐⭐⭐ **Complete the sentences.**

	Suzy and Kelly	Mr Brown and Mrs Simm
Rory		Ben
_It_ is a pen.	¹ _____ is Suzy.	⁴ _____ are teachers.
The pen is _Rory's_ pen.	Suzy is ² _____ friend.	Mr Brown and Mrs Simm are ⁵ _____ teachers.
The pen is _his_ pen.	Suzy is ³ _____ friend.	Mr Brown and Mrs Simm are ⁶ _____ teachers.

Object pronouns

5 ⭐⭐ **Choose the correct answers.**

You're next to the board. You're next to _____.

a it   b them   c him   d us

1 The teacher is near James and Sarah.
  She's near _____.
  a it   b them   c her   d him
2 Isabel is with Tom. She's with _____.
  a them   b it   c us   d him
3 The dictionaries are next to me and Emma.
  The dictionaries are next to _____.
  a it   b them   c us   d him
4 The books are near you and Charlie.
  The books are near _____.
  a it   b us   c her   d you
5 You're in class with Maria. You're with _____.
  a her   b it   c you   d us
6 I'm here in France. Lily is with _____.
  a her   b me   c you   d them

VOCABULARY ■ Basic adjectives

1 ⭐ **Complete the adjectives in the sentences.**

This bag is very exp<u>e n s i v e</u>.

1 My favourite football team is unp _ _ _ _ _ _!
2 My pizza is hor _ _ _ _ _!
3 Ben's new laptop is very sm _ _ _.
4 This DVD is bor _ _ _.
5 Her book is dif _ _ _ _ _ _.
6 This video game is b _ _.

2 ⭐⭐ **Complete the crossword with the opposite of the adjectives in exercise 1.**

```
C H E A ¹P
         │
         │
         │
² _      ³ _
⁴ _ _ ⁵ _ _ _ _ ⁶ _
         │
         │
```

3 ⭐⭐ **Look at the pictures and complete the sentences.**

She's __popular__.

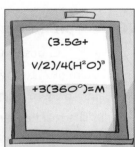

1 It's _____.

2 The laptop is _____.

3 It's _____.

4 The film is _____.

5 The car is _____.

6 The TV programme is _____.

7 Lucy's bag is _____.

4 ⭐⭐⭐ **Describe the people, places and things. Use *be* and adjectives in exercises 1 and 2.**

My teacher _____ *is popular* _____.

1 London _____.
2 English _____.
3 Johnny Depp _____.
4 My best friend _____.
5 My book _____.
6 My school _____.
7 Football _____.
8 New York _____.

Days of the week and months

5 ⭐⭐ **Complete the days of the week and the months.**

Days

¹ <u>Monday</u> Tuesday ² _____ Thursday
³ _____ Saturday ⁴ _____

Months

January ⁵ _____ March ⁶ _____ May
⁷ _____ July ⁸ _____ September
⁹ _____ November ¹⁰ _____

LANGUAGE FOCUS ◼ *be*: affirmative, negative and questions

1 ⭐ Complete the table with the words in the box.

> aren't   's   Am   'm not   Is   're
> 'm   isn't   Are

Affirmative

I ¹ **'m** eleven years old.
He / She / It ² _____ nice.
You / We / You / They ³ _____ interesting.

Negative

I ⁴ _____ from France.
He / She / It ⁵ _____ unpopular.
You / We / You / They ⁶ _____ fifteen years old.

Questions

⁷ _____ I next to Emily?
⁸ _____ he / she / it popular?
⁹ _____ you / we / you / they from Italy?

2 ⭐⭐ Complete the sentences with *'m, 's* or *'re*.

I **'m** _____ a really good student.

1 You _____ very popular!
2 She _____ next to the window.
3 They _____ in London now.
4 It _____ a boring DVD!
5 I _____ from Liverpool.
6 We _____ in the new classroom.
7 He _____ thirteen years old today.

3 ⭐⭐ Rewrite the sentences using the negative form.

I'm English.

I'm not English. _____

1 The video games are very popular.
_____

2 They're fourteen years old.
_____

3 The teacher's car is expensive.
_____

4 The CD player is in the classroom.
_____

5 You're in my class.
_____

6 We're from Rome.
_____

7 English is a difficult language.
_____

4 ⭐⭐ Look at the photos and write questions and short answers.

__Are__ you next to the window?
__No, I'm not.__

1 _____ it small?
_____

2 _____ the bags on the desk?
_____

3 _____ the laptop cheap?
_____

4 _____ the DVDs in the bag?
_____

5 _____ the exercise easy?
_____

5 ⭐⭐⭐ Complete the interview using the correct form of *be*.

Jack   _____ **Are** _____ you a student, Toby?
Toby   Yes, I ¹ _____.
Jack   ² _____ you twelve years old?
Toby   No, I ³ _____, I ⁴ _____ thirteen.
Jack   ⁵ _____ your school interesting?
Toby   Yes, it ⁶ _____. But it ⁷ _____ easy.
Jack   ⁸ _____ your teachers nice?
Toby   Yes, they ⁹ _____. They ¹⁰ _____ very interesting. They ¹¹ _____ boring!
Jack   ¹² _____ you and your friends good students?
Toby   Yes, we ¹³ _____! We ¹⁴ _____ really nice!

VOCABULARY ◼ Free time

1 (★) **Find eleven more interests.**

I	N	T	E	R	N	E	T	Z	W	U	Q	L	C
C	O	M	P	U	T	E	R	G	A	M	E	S	Y
X	M	A	R	T	I	A	L	A	R	T	S	B	C
S	U	O	K	A	N	I	M	A	L	S	E	O	L
P	S	T	V	R	P	B	Y	F	Q	T	N	O	I
O	I	W	A	T	C	H	I	N	G	T	V	K	N
R	C	Y	Z	A	Q	Y	Z	C	E	X	K	S	G
T	Q	P	H	O	T	O	G	R	A	P	H	Y	W
M	E	E	T	I	N	G	F	R	I	E	N	D	S

_____ internet

1 _____
2 _____
3 _____
4 _____
5 _____
6 _____
7 _____
8 _____
9 _____
10 _____
11 _____

2 (★★) **Complete the words in the text.**

Hi, my name's Ella and I'm 13. I'm into
m<u>usic</u> and ¹b_____. I prefer
²m_____ friends to ³c_____
on the internet, and I'm really into
⁴c_____, too. My brother Max is 15.
He loves ⁵w_____ TV and playing
⁶c_____ games. He likes
⁷p_____, too. He isn't interested
in ⁸s_____ and he really hates
⁹m_____ a_____.

3 (★★) **Write sentences with the words in exercise 1.**

I'm interested in ____animals____.

1 I like 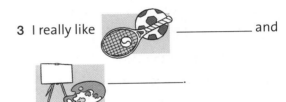 _____ and

 _____.

2 I'm not into [music notes] _____.

3 I really like [tennis/football] _____ and

[art] _____.

4 I'm not very interested in [TV/games console]

_____ _____.

4 (★★★) **What are your interests? Use the words in exercise 1 and the phrases in exercise 3 to write true sentences about you.**

<u>I'm interested in computer games and chatting on</u>
<u>the internet.</u>

1 _____
_____
2 _____
_____
3 _____
_____
4 _____
_____
5 _____
_____
6 _____
_____

have got

1 ⭐ Complete the table with the words in the box.

> has   haven't   Have   hasn't   Has   ~~have~~

Affirmative
I / You / We / You / They ¹ __have__ got a CD by *U2*. He / She ² _____ got a DVD about animals.

Negative
I / You / We / You / They ³ _____ got an art book. He / She ⁴ _____ got a poster of New York.

Questions
⁵ _____ I / you / we / you / they got a camera? ⁶ _____ he / she got a good computer game?

2 ⭐⭐ Write affirmative or negative sentences using *have got*.

I / three computer games

__I've got three computer games.__

1 they / a new CD

_____

2 my brother / not / a bike

_____

3 we / not / a laptop

_____

4 Ann and James / a big dog

_____

5 I / not / a notebook in my bag

_____

6 my friend / a good camera

_____

3 ⭐⭐ Write questions and short answers using *have got*.

you / CD player ✗

__Have you got a CD player? No, I haven't.__

1 the teacher / a bike ✗ _____

_____

2 Daniel / an interesting book ✓ _____

3 we / a nice teacher ✓ _____

_____

4 they / an English dictionary ✗ _____

_____

5 you / a big poster ✓ _____

_____

6 Angela / a sister ✗ _____

_____

Prepositions: *about, of, by*

4 ⭐⭐ What has Ben got? Look at the list and write *He's got* or *He hasn't got*. Then complete the sentences with *about, of* or *by*.

cycling DVD ✓
Dizzee Rascal CD ✓
photography book ✗
Rihanna CD ✗
Bart Simpson poster ✓

__He's got__ a DVD __about__ cycling.

1 _____ a CD _____ Dizzee Rascal.

2 _____ a book _____ photography.

3 _____ a CD _____ Rihanna.

4 _____ a poster _____ Bart Simpson.

5 ⭐⭐⭐ Write true affirmative and negative sentences using *have got / haven't got* or *has got / hasn't got*.

My mother ____ __has got a book about animals.__

My father ____ __hasn't got a CD by the Sugababes.__

1 I _____.

2 We _____.

3 My teacher _____.

4 My best friend _____.

5 My cousin _____.

6 My school friends _____.

VOCABULARY ■ Hobbies and interests

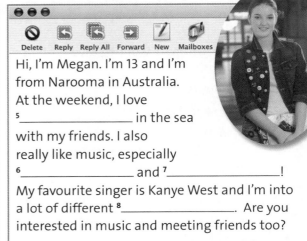

1 ⭐ **Choose the correct words.**

Charlie is really into football. His favourite (team)/ **player** is Manchester United.

1 I'm a big fan of the film **actors** / **players** Johnny Depp and Angelina Jolie.
2 My Dad loves computers. He's got a new white **programme** / **laptop** in his bag.
3 My sister has got a guitar and she's in a **group** / **team.**
4 My brother is interested in martial arts. He's into karate **websites** / **programmes** on the internet.
5 I like all the Harry Potter books. The **films** / **groups** are good too.
6 I'm mad about Lady Gaga. She's a fantastic **singer** / **director**.

2 ⭐⭐ **Complete the emails with the words in the box.**

> actor   programme   films   ~~sport~~   hip hop   swimming   classical   player   groups

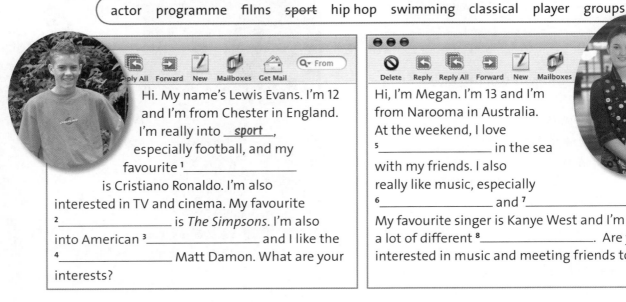

Reply All   Forward   New   Mailboxes   Get Mail   Q▾ From

Hi. My name's Lewis Evans. I'm 12 and I'm from Chester in England. I'm really into __sport__, especially football, and my favourite ¹_____ is Cristiano Ronaldo. I'm also interested in TV and cinema. My favourite ²_____ is *The Simpsons*. I'm also into American ³_____ and I like the ⁴_____ Matt Damon. What are your interests?

Delete   Reply   Reply All   Forward   New   Mailboxes

Hi, I'm Megan. I'm 13 and I'm from Narooma in Australia. At the weekend, I love ⁵_____ in the sea with my friends. I also really like music, especially ⁶_____ and ⁷_____! My favourite singer is Kanye West and I'm into a lot of different ⁸_____. Are you interested in music and meeting friends too?

3 ⭐⭐ **Replace the word which doesn't match with a word from the box.**

> team   actor   ~~swimming~~   singer   laptop

tennis   ~~mouse~~   football   cricket
__swimming__

1 skiing   guitar   hip hop   band
   _____

2 programme   film   team   director
   _____

3 website   mouse   drummer   webcam
   _____

4 player   science fiction   referee   match
   _____

4 ⭐⭐⭐ **Write a word group for one of your interests. For example: animals, art, books or TV.**

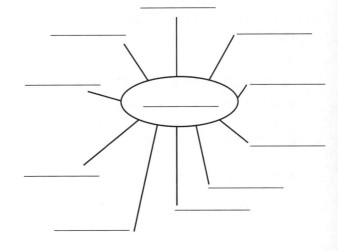

Interrogative pronouns

1 ⭐ Complete the questions with the words in the box. Then match questions 1–6 with answers a–f.

> What ~~Where~~ How many Who
> When How

1 ___Where___ are you from?
2 _____'s your name?
3 _____'s your favourite actor?
4 _____ old are you?
5 _____'s your birthday?
6 _____ brothers and sisters have you got?

a Robert.
b Canada.
c Two.
d 10th November.
e George Clooney.
f Twelve.

2 ⭐⭐ Complete the quiz questions. Then choose the correct answers.

QUIZ

___How many___ players are in a hockey team?

a seven **|b eleven|** c fifteen

1 _____ is the footballer Lionel Messi from?

a Argentina b France c Italy

2 _____ is the sport of basketball?

a 40 years old **b** 80 years old
c 120 years old

3 _____ is the Wimbledon tennis tournament?

a April b June c September

4 _____ is the name of the Manchester United football stadium?

a Stamford Bridge b Anfield
c Old Trafford

5 _____ is the sister of tennis player Venus Williams?

a Serena b Marina c Katrina

6 _____ players are in a basketball team?

a four b five c six

3 ⭐⭐⭐ Complete the questions. Then write answers that are true for you.

___Where's___ your school?

It's _____

1 _____ your name?
_____

2 _____ your birthday?
_____

3 _____ your favourite colour?
_____

4 _____ your favourite pop star?
_____

5 _____ old is your best friend?
_____

6 _____ many CDs have you got?
_____

this, that, these, those

4 ⭐⭐ Look at the pictures and complete the sentences with *This, That, These* or *Those*.

___This___ is my new friend, George.

1 _____ camera is very expensive!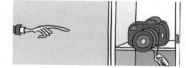

2 _____ are my friends, Jessica and Kate.

3 _____ computer game is very good!

4 _____ photo is really cool.

5 _____ boys are from my school.

Favourite things

I'm a music fan and my favourite thing is an old CD by Kylie Minogue. It's called *Fever*. I've got sixty pop and hip hop CDs but *Fever* is my favourite.

A Simon

What's my favourite thing? My bike! I'm really into cycling. I've got a fantastic bike – it's old but it's very good. I like cycling in the mountains with my friends. I'm interested in sport, especially tennis. I'm a big Wimbledon fan.

B Karen

C Lulu and Anna

We're mad about animals and we've got a dog called Ollie. He's our favourite 'thing'! We're also into photography. We've got hundreds of photos of Ollie on the computer and he's got his own website – *Ollie's World*.

---

1 ★ Read the text. Who has got a website about their favourite thing?

_____

2 ★★ Read the text again. Match topics 1–5 with paragraphs A–C.

animals _____C_____

1 pop music _____
2 cycling _____
3 a singer _____
4 sport _____
5 photography _____

3 ★★ Read the text again. Are the sentences *true* or *false* ?

Simon is into cycling. _____true_____

1 Simon's bike is new. _____
2 Simon likes Wimbledon. _____
3 Karen has got a hundred CDs. _____
4 Karen is into pop music. _____
5 Lulu and Anna are interested in photography. _____
6 *Ollie's World* is the name of a book. _____

4 ★★★ Answer the questions. Write complete sentences.

What are Simon's interests?

His interests are cycling and tennis.

1 What has Simon got?

_____

2 What's Karen's favourite thing?

_____

3 How many CDs has Karen got?

_____

4 What are Lulu and Anna mad about?

_____

5 What's the name of Lulu and Anna's dog?

_____

6 How many photos of the dog have Lulu and Anna got?

_____

Build your vocabulary

5 ★★ Match sentence halves 1–6 with a–f.

1 I'm mad   a stand football.
2 He's good   b fan.
3 We can't   c about music.
4 She's a Taylor Lautner   d prefer computers.
5 I'm not into books. I   e drawing.
6 He likes art, especially   f at photography.

WRITING ▪ A description of someone

Language point: and, or, but

1 ⭐ **Choose the correct words.**

I like cycling (but) / or I haven't got a bike.

1 My dad is into drawing **and** / **but** watching films on TV.
2 Laura has got her laptop **and** / **but** she hasn't got her mobile phone.
3 Do you prefer cycling **but** / **or** running?
4 I've got two hobbies – tennis **and** / **or** swimming.
5 I'm not mad about computer games **but** / **or** chatting on the internet.
6 I can't stand sport **or** / **but** I like art.

2 ⭐⭐ **Complete the sentences.**

I've got two white cats and ___a black dog___ .

1 She's interested in photography but _____
_____.
2 We're into Manga comics and _____
_____.
3 I'm not mad about rock or _____
_____.
4 Peter hasn't got a sister but _____
_____.
5 Do you prefer blue or _____
_____.
6 He's mad about skiing and _____
_____.
7 I'm not interested in classical music or _____
_____.

◯ TASK

3 ⭐⭐ **Read the notes about Orlando Bloom. Then complete the text.**

Fact file

Name:	Orlando Bloom
From:	Canterbury, UK
Family:	a sister, Samantha
Pets:	two dogs, Essa and Sidi
Hobbies:	surfing, snowboarding
Not interested in:	computers, the internet
Favourite actors:	Johnny Depp, Brad Pitt
Favourite food:	pizza or pasta

All about Orlando ...

Orlando Bloom is a famous actor and he's in the film *Pirates of the Caribbean*. Orlando has got a lot of fans in different countries. <u>He's from Canterbury</u>, a small city in the UK.

¹_____ and her name's Samantha. He's mad about animals and
²_____.
Their names are Essa and Sidi. He's also into sport – he likes ³_____,
⁴_____,
computers or chatting to people on the internet. He prefers meeting his friends in a café.

At home, Orlando likes watching films or DVDs – his favourite actors are
⁵_____.

He likes Italian restaurants and he usually prefers
⁶_____.

4 ⭐⭐⭐ **Write about a brother, sister or friend. Use the text in exercise 3 to help you.**

PROGRESS REVIEW ● Unit 1

VOCABULARY ● Free time

1 Complete the sentences with the words in the box.

> chatting   sport   watching   photography
> meeting   cycling   music

1 Jack is into _____, especially football.
2 I love _____ on the internet with my friends.
3 Jessica likes _____. She's got a new bike.
4 He's got a camera. He's mad about _____.
5 We hate _____ TV. It's boring.
6 I like _____ my friends in the café.
7 She isn't interested in _____ and she really hates hip hop.

> **I can talk about my hobbies and interests.**
> MY EVALUATION   ◻◻◻◻

READING ● What are you into?

2 Complete the dialogue with the words in the box.

> mad   fan   especially   good   prefer
> can't stand

Adam My brother's really ¹_____ at sport, ²_____ volleyball. What about you?

Ollie Volleyball? It's very difficult – I ³_____ it! I ⁴_____ basketball – it's really easy.

Adam Yes, my sister is ⁵_____ about basketball. She's a Harlem Globetrotter's ⁶_____. They're a very popular team.

> **I can understand a text about people's interests.**
> MY EVALUATION   ◻◻◻◻

LANGUAGE FOCUS ● have got

3 Look at the table. Then complete the sentences with *has got, have got, hasn't got, haven't got*.

	dog	camera	laptop
Cara	✓	✗	✓
Ben and Sam	✗	✓	✗

1 Cara _____ a dog.
2 Ben and Sam _____ a laptop.
3 Cara _____ a camera.
4 Ben and Sam _____ a dog.
5 Cara _____ a laptop.
6 Ben and Sam _____ a camera.

> **I can talk about possessions.**
> MY EVALUATION   ◻◻◻◻

VOCABULARY AND LISTENING ● Hobbies and interests

4 Choose the correct answers.

1 I've got CDs by Leona Lewis and Beyoncé. They're really good _____.
   a players   b singers   c actors   d directors
2 He's mad about music. He's in a hip hop _____.
   a match   b team   c group   d programme
3 Our school has got a _____ on the internet.
   a website   b mouse   c email   d director
4 She likes _____ films. *Star Wars* is her favourite.
   a classical   b hip hop   c science fiction   d match
5 The football _____ is on Saturday.
   a group   b match   c player   d camera
6 I've got _____ from my friend.
   a an email   b a website   c a programme   d a mouse

> **I can understand people talking about their hobbies and interests.**
> MY EVALUATION   ◻◻◻◻

LANGUAGE FOCUS ■ Interrogative pronouns

5 Read the answers and complete the questions with an interrogative pronoun.

1 _____'s your father from?
Portugal.

2 _____'s the English exam?
On Thursday.

3 _____ are you?
Eleven.

4 _____ brothers have you got?
Two.

5 _____'s your favourite DVD?
Titanic.

6 _____'s your best friend?
Michael.

> **I can ask and answer general knowledge questions.**
>
> MY EVALUATION ☐☐☐☐

SPEAKING ■ Meeting people

6 Complete the dialogue with the phrases in the box.

> How are things   See you later then
> Good to meet you   What part of Australia
> This is Sam   Are you into photography

Maria Hello, Karl.
¹_____?

Karl Not bad, thanks.
²_____. He's
my cousin. He's from Australia.

Maria Hi, Sam.
³_____.

Sam And you. Hey, that's a cool camera.
⁴_____?

Maria Yes, but I'm not very good at it.
⁵_____ are
you from?

Sam I'm from Sydney.

Maria That's interesting.
⁶_____.

Sam Yeah. See you later.

> **I can greet and introduce people.**
>
> MY EVALUATION ☐☐☐☐

WRITING ■ An email

7 Choose the correct answers in these sentences from an email.

1 Hi! I'm a student _____ Seaford School.
   a for **b** at **c** about **d** into

2 I'm really _____ pop music.
   a about **b** for **c** into **d** to

3 I like sport and I'm good _____ hockey.
   a to **b** for **c** about **d** at

4 What _____ you?
   a about **b** if **c** for **d** into

5 Send a photo _____ you've got one.
   a for **b** at **c** about **d** if

6 Bye _____ now!
   a to **b** for **c** at **d** into

> **I can write an email about myself.**
>
> MY EVALUATION ☐☐☐☐

2 ▪▫▫▫▫▫▫▫ City to city

VOCABULARY ▪ Places in a town

1 ⭐ Look at the pictures and choose the correct words.

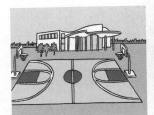

~~sports centre~~ / shopping centre

1 café / cinema

2 restaurant / shop

3 factory / hospital

4 car park / school

5 train station / library

2 ⭐⭐ Complete the words in the sentences.

She's got a very bad leg. She's in h <u>o s p i t a l</u>.

1 My dog loves swimming. He's in the r _ _ _ _.
2 They're o _ _ _ _ _ _. They aren't shops.
3 We haven't got any milk. We're at the s _ _ _ _ _ _ _ _ _ _.
4 He's interested in Picasso. He's at the a _ _ g _ _ _ _ _ _.
5 We're in my f _ _ _. It's near my school.
6 The b _ _ s _ _ _ _ _ _ is in town.
7 There aren't any cars in the c _ _ p _ _ _.
8 The s _ _ _ _ _ _ _ c _ _ _ _ _ is near the train station.

3 ⭐⭐ Look at the picture. Write four more sentences about places you can see and four sentences about places you can't see.

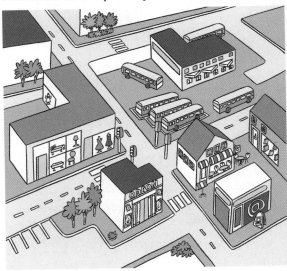

<u>There's a café.</u>

1 _____
2 _____
3 _____
4 _____
5 _____
6 _____
7 _____
8 _____

4 ⭐⭐⭐ Complete the sentences about your town.

My town has got _____ <u>a bus station</u> _____.

1 My house is near _____.
2 My school is next to _____.
3 There's a _____ in my town.
4 There isn't a _____.
5 There aren't any _____.
6 There are some _____.
7 My mum likes the library, but I prefer _____ _____.
8 The shops _____ _____.

there is, there are + a, an, some and *any*

1 ⭐ Complete the table with the words in the box.

> aren't a isn't any i̶s̶ an are some

Affirmative	
Singular	**Plural**
There ¹ _is_ ² _____ park near here.	There ³ _____ ⁴ _____ people in the library.
Negative	
Singular	**Plural**
There ⁵ _____ ⁶ _____ art gallery.	There ⁷ _____ ⁸ _____ shops here.

2 ⭐⭐ Write affirmative ✓ and negative ✗ sentences using *there is / there are*. Use *a, an, some* or *any*.

supermarket ✓

There's a supermarket.

1 schools ✓

2 cafés ✗

3 restaurant near the cinema ✗

4 library next to the supermarket ✓

5 car parks ✗

6 train station ✓

7 shops at the train station ✗

8 offices near the park ✓

9 cinema near the shops ✓

10 art gallery ✗

Is there ...?, Are there ...?

3 ⭐⭐ Write questions and answers.

supermarket / yes

Is there a supermarket?   Yes, there is.

restaurants / three

How many restaurants are there?

There are three.

1 schools / two

2 cafés / no

3 flats / yes

4 library / no

5 shops / four

6 art gallery / yes

4 ⭐⭐⭐ Write questions and sentences using words from the lists.

two	park	in my town
a	shops	in your town
many	libraries	near the school
an	office	next to the park
any	schools	where I live
some	cinemas	where you live
four	restaurant	are there
three	art gallery	near the shops

Are there any cinemas where you live?

1 Are there _____?
2 Is there _____?
3 How _____?
4 How _____?
5 There are _____.
6 There is _____.
7 There aren't _____.
8 There isn't _____.

VOCABULARY ■ Describing places

1 ★ Find seven more adjectives. Write the adjectives under positive 😊 or negative 😞.

Q	U	I	E	T	U	N	Z	L	Y
K	A	S	C	V	Q	O	Y	P	S
Y	D	I	R	T	Y	I	E	R	A
H	C	J	E	B	W	S	H	E	O
U	G	L	Y	N	X	Y	O	T	N
B	F	A	Q	S	K	P	Z	T	D
W	C	L	E	A	N	T	C	Y	E
V	E	X	M	F	U	J	T	L	R
D	A	N	G	E	R	O	U	S	T
C	L	E	E	N	O	R	F	L	I

Positive 😊   Negative 😞

____quiet____   _____

_____   _____

_____   _____

_____   _____

2 ★★ Look at the picture and correct the adjectives.

My school is a very ~~modern~~ *old* building. Our classroom is really clean and the students are very quiet — it's very safe at the moment! My teacher is quite ugly, and she's really nice and unfriendly.

3 ★★ Look at the pictures and complete the sentences with an adjective.

The office is quite ____dirty____.

1 The library is very _____.

2 The people aren't very _____.

3 The shop is really _____.

4 The park is really _____.

5 The buildings in the city are very _____.

4 ★★★ Complete the sentences with adjectives from exercise 1 and *very*, *quite* and *really*.

I live in ____a very modern, friendly city____.

1 I live on a _____ street.
2 My house / flat is _____.
3 My school is a _____ building.
4 The students are _____.
5 The shopping centre near my house / flat is

_____.
6 The park in my town is _____.
7 The supermarket isn't _____.
8 The library in my school is _____.

Comparative adjectives

1 (★) **Write the comparative forms of the adjectives in the box.**

> bad big ~~clean~~ dangerous dirty
> good popular pretty quiet safe
> far expensive

Short adjectives
cleaner

Long adjectives

Irregular

2 (★★) **Complete each sentence so that it means the same as the first sentence. Use the comparative form of the adjectives in brackets.**

London is bigger than Paris. (small)

Paris is smaller than London.

1 The library is older than the cinema. (modern)
  The cinema _____
  _____ .

2 The bus station is nearer than the train station. (far)
  The train station _____
  _____ .

3 These houses are more expensive than those flats. (cheap)
  Those flats _____
  _____ .

4 Geneva is quieter than New York. (noisy)
  New York _____
  _____ .

5 The sports centre is cleaner than the shopping centre. (dirty)
  The shopping centre _____
  _____ .

6 The swimming pool is safer than the river. (dangerous)
  The river _____
  _____ .

3 (★★★) **Read the description of two towns, Weston and Kinton. Then write sentences about them using the comparative form of the adjectives.**

> Weston isn't a nice town. It isn't clean, and it's very noisy and dangerous. In Weston, people are really unfriendly. Weston is an ugly town, but its flats aren't very expensive.
>
> Kinton is a really pretty town and it isn't noisy. It's safe and clean too, and the people are really friendly. But it isn't cheap. Flats in Kinton are really expensive!

(noisy) Weston is noisier than Kinton.

1 (quiet) _____
2 (clean) _____
3 (dangerous) _____
4 (safe) _____
5 (ugly) _____
6 (cheap) _____
7 (expensive) _____
8 (friendly) _____

Prepositions: *by* and *on*

4 (★★) **Complete the sentences with *by* or *on*.**

It's cheaper __by__ bus.

1 A return ticket _____ the train is £15.20.
2 Paris is two hours from here _____ plane.
3 It's about twenty minutes to the shops _____ car.
4 How much is a single ticket _____ the coach?
5 It's more dangerous on foot than _____ car.
6 The park is an hour from here _____ foot.
7 Maria is _____ the plane now.
8 I really hate travelling _____ train.

5 (★★) **Complete the dialogue with *by* or *on*.**

Woman Good morning. Can I help you?
Dylan Yes, I want to visit Liverpool __by__ coach or ¹_____ train.
Woman It's only two hours from here ²_____ the train. It's faster ³_____ train than ⁴_____ coach.
Dylan That's interesting.
Woman And the station isn't far. It's ten minutes from here ⁵_____ foot or two minutes ⁶_____ the bus.
Dylan Great. Thanks very much.

READING ● A description of a place

1 ⭐ **Read the text. Tick ✓ the correct box.**

Dan's ideal place is …

a ☐ London   b ☐ The British Isles   c ☐ Sark

A I'm from London, but I live on Sark, an island in the British Isles.

B London is a fantastic city; it's really big, with amazing buildings and luxury shops, but it's noisy. I'm not into cities – I prefer quieter places.

C Sark is tiny, 5.45 km², and its population is small too. There are only about 600 people on the island. There are some small shops and restaurants, one or two offices and one school. But the incredible thing is there are no cars!

D Sark is ideal for cycling, and it's a popular place for tourists. It's really pretty and there are a lot of animals.

E I'm interested in cycling and photography, not shopping or fast cars. That's why my home is here in Sark, not London. It's the perfect place for me.

---

2 ⭐⭐ **Read the text again. Match topics 1–4 with paragraphs A–E.**

About the island ___C___

1 Why Dan likes Sark _____
2 Why people are interested in visiting Sark _____
3 Where Dan lives _____
4 About London _____

3 ⭐⭐ **Read the text again. Choose the correct answers.**

Dan lives _____.

a in a city
(b on a small island)
c on a big island

1 Sark has got a population of _____ people.
  a 60   b 545   c 600
2 On Sark there aren't any _____.
  a shops   b cars   c restaurants
3 The island has got a _____.
  a school   b tourist office   c luxury shop
4 On Sark there are a lot of _____.
  a incredible buildings   b animals   c cities
5 The island is popular with _____.
  a boys   b people from London   c tourists
6 Dan _____ Sark.
  a loves   b quite likes   c hates

4 ⭐⭐⭐ **Answer the questions. Write complete sentences.**

Where does Dan live?

He lives on Sark, an island in the British Isles.

1 Why does Dan think London is a good place to live?
  _____
  _____

2 Why doesn't Dan like living in cities?
  _____
  _____

3 How big is Sark?
  _____

4 What is special about Sark?
  _____

5 What do tourists like doing on Sark?
  _____

6 What is Dan interested in?
  _____

Build your vocabulary

5 ⭐⭐ **Look at the words in brackets. Then complete the text with the words in the box.**

tiny   ~~fantastic~~   fast   incredible
enormous   amazing   luxury

Ruth has got a ___fantastic___ (very good) job. She's got an ¹_____ (very big) office in the centre of London. Her office is bigger than my flat! It's in an ²_____ (very beautiful and big) building.

Ruth has got a ³_____ (very expensive and beautiful) flat near the park and a new car – it's really ⁴_____ (very quick)! It's an ⁵_____ (very surprising) car. I love it! She's got a ⁶_____ (very small) dog – his name is Benji.

Language point: Position of adjectives

1 ⭐ Rewrite the sentences with the adjective in the correct place.

I've got a car. (expensive)

<u>I've got an expensive car.</u>

1 The Burj Khalifa is a building. (spectacular)

_____

_____

2 This is a train station. (very old)

_____

3 There's a park near here. (pretty)

_____

4 My school is next to some flats. (luxury)

_____

_____

5 There are some girls at my school. (really unfriendly)

_____

_____

6 Max has got a dog. (really noisy)

_____

_____

2 ⭐⭐ Order the words to make sentences.

dirty / I'm / bus station / a / in

<u>I'm in a dirty bus station.</u>

1 car / really / Jason / got / a / expensive / has

_____

_____

2 a lot of / my / there are / friendly / people / town / in

_____

_____

3 exciting / New York / really / is / city / a

_____

_____

4 modern / library / in / the / building / is / a

_____

_____

5 city / pretty / there / is / a / the / park / near / centre

_____

_____

6 got / you've / really / a / flat / modern

_____

_____

○ TASK

3 ⭐⭐ Read Paul's information about Newcastle. Then complete the text.

Favourite city: Newcastle

Location: north-east of England

Distance from London: 400 kilometres

Population: 280,000

Facilities: parks, modern shopping centres

Advantages: good for shopping

Football team: Newcastle United

City: really exciting

People: very friendly

Hi, I'm Paul and my favourite city is <u>Newcastle</u>. It's in the ¹_____
_____ and it's
²_____ from
London. It's quite a big city and there are
³_____
people living there. There are ⁴_____
_____ and it's a great place
⁵_____. Newcastle
has got ⁶_____
– Newcastle United. I'm one of their fans!
Newcastle is a ⁷_____
and the people are ⁸_____.

4 ⭐⭐⭐ Write a description of a city. Use the text in exercise 3 to help you.

MY EVALUATION   Check your progress. Do the exercises and then complete your own evaluation.

▣◻◻◻ I need to try this again.   ▣▣▣◻ I am happy with this.

▣▣◻◻ I could do this better.   ▣▣▣▣ I can do this very well.

VOCABULARY ● Places in a town

1 Complete the words in the sentences.

1 There's a good film at the c _ _ _ _ _.
2 This Italian r _ _ _ _ _ _ _ _ _ is expensive!
3 There are a lot of books in this l _ _ _ _ _ _.
4 Ben loves tennis – he's at the s _ _ _ _ _
   c _ _ _ _ _ now.
5 We haven't got any coffee. Please go to the
   s _ _ _ _ for me.
6 My father is at work. He's in one of those big
   o _ _ _ _ _ _.
7 Where's your car? It's in the c _ _ p _ _ _.
8 My mother is a doctor at the h _ _ _ _ _ _ _.
9 We haven't got a car – we go to the b _ _
   s _ _ _ _ _ _ every day.
10 I'm a student at the High s _ _ _ _ _ near here.

> **I can describe a town I know.**
> MY EVALUATION ◻◻◻◻

READING ● A description of a modern city

2 Choose the correct answers.

1 My favourite city is Tokyo. It's _____.
   a luxury b amazing c tiny
2 The film stars are in a _____ hotel in
   London. It's very expensive.
   a enormous b incredible c luxury
3 Your new poster is really big. It's _____.
   a enormous b tiny c fast
4 That book is very interesting. It's _____.
   a luxury b fantastic c fast
5 Your dog is really small. It's _____.
   a luxury b enormous c tiny
6 The trains are very _____. It's only 30
   minutes to London from here.
   a fast b enormous c tiny
7 The library has got 50,000 books – it's _____.
   a luxury b incredible c fast

> **I can understand an article about a city.**
> MY EVALUATION ◻◻◻◻

LANGUAGE FOCUS ● Is there ...?, Are there ...?

3 Look at the table and write questions and short answers.

shops	three	libraries	two
schools	✓	hospital	✗
park	✗	internet café	✓

1 How many _____? There are _____.
2 Are there _____? Yes, _____.
3 Is there _____
4 _____
5 _____
6 _____

> **I can ask and answer questions about my ideal place to live.**
> MY EVALUATION ◻◻◻◻

VOCABULARY AND LISTENING ● Describing places

4 Complete the dialogues with the adjectives in the box.

> old   dangerous   noisy   unfriendly
> clean   ugly

1 This park is quite dirty.
   No, it isn't. It's really _____.
2 My city is very modern.
   Well, my town is _____.
3 Cycling in this town is safe.
   Safe! It's really _____.
4 The shopping centre is nice and quiet today.
   No, it isn't! It's very _____.
5 That new art gallery is pretty.
   No, it isn't. It's _____.
6 The people in the café are friendly.
   But they're really _____ to me!

> **I can understand descriptions and describe where I live.**
> MY EVALUATION ◻◻◻◻

LANGUAGE FOCUS ■ Comparative adjectives

5 Complete the sentences with the adjectives in the box. Use the comparative form.

> dangerous long expensive tall
> clean unfriendly pretty noisy

1 The Empire State Building is
_____ than the Eiffel Tower.

2 The River Nile is _____ than the
River Thames.

3 Is your town _____ than New
York? No, it's really safe.

4 That plane ticket to Rome is 1,000 euros! It's
_____ than the train.

5 This park is beautiful. It's _____
than the ugly park near my home.

6 The air in my town is _____
than the air in this city.

7 London is _____ than my
village. My village is quiet!

8 The people in your town are
_____ than the people in my
town.

> **I can compare places in different countries.**
>
> MY EVALUATION ☐ ☐ ☐ ☐

SPEAKING ■ Asking for travel information

6 Put the dialogue in the correct order. Number the sentences.

a ☐ **Adam** Yes, please. I want to visit Edinburgh. How far is it from here?

b ☐ **Man** Hello. Can I help you?

c ☐ **Adam** OK. Thanks very much.

d ☐ **Man** A return ticket is £50. The coaches are cheaper.

e ☐ **Adam** How much is a return train ticket?

f ☐ **Man** It's about 90 minutes from here on the train.

> **I can ask for travel information.**
>
> MY EVALUATION ☐ ☐ ☐ ☐

WRITING ■ A description of a town

7 Order the words to make sentences.

1 is / Bristol / exciting / city / very / a

_____

_____

2 west / of / it's / the / England / in

_____

_____

3 population / got / of / a / 500,000 / it's /

_____

_____

4 favourite / place / my / art gallery / is / the

_____

_____

5 are / great / there / shops / some

_____

_____

6 football / it's / two / teams / got

_____

_____

7 like / I / Bristol / it's / because / place / friendly / a

_____

_____

8 kilometres / about / it's / 190 / London / from

_____

_____

> **I can write about a town or city I like.**
>
> MY EVALUATION ☐ ☐ ☐ ☐

3 ⬤▫▫▫▫◻◻◻◻ Around the world

VOCABULARY ▪ Countries, nationalities and languages

1 ⭐ Complete the crossword.

ACROSS grid with **J A P A N E S E** (4 across) and **N** (8 down).

ACROSS

4 Hiroko is from Japan. He's ... .
5 Joey is from the USA. He's ... .
6 Ye Ming is from China. He's ... .
9 Kim and Tyler are from Canada. They're ... .
10 Carla is from Italy. She's ... .
11 Eva is from Poland. She's ... .

DOWN

1 Karl and Heidi are from Germany. They're ... .
2 Jean Claude is from France. He's ... .
3 Luiz is from Brazil. He's ... .
7 Diego and Jaime are from Spain. They're ... .
8 Tom is from the UK. He's ... .

2 ⭐⭐ Complete the sentences with the words in the box.

~~German~~	Spanish
American	Australia
Germany	Spain
Australian	the UK

Claudia Schiffer is ___German___.

1 Barack Obama is _____.
2 Michael Schumacher is from _____.
3 Nicole Kidman is _____.
4 Penelope Cruz is from _____.
5 Robert Pattinson is from _____.
6 Kylie Minogue is from _____.
7 Rafael Nadal is _____.

3 ⭐⭐ Complete the sentences. Write the country, nationality or language.

Toledo and Granada are in ___Spain___.

1 Keiko is from Japan. She speaks _____.
2 Ottawa is the capital of _____.
3 Paris and Toulouse are in _____.
4 Artur is Polish. He's from _____.
5 Beijing is the capital city of _____.
6 Pizza and spaghetti are famous _____ foods.
7 The 2012 Olympics are in London, in _____.
8 Rio de Janeiro and Brasilia are in _____.

4 ⭐⭐⭐ Complete the sentences with countries, nationalities or languages.

My mother speaks ___French and German___.

1 I speak _____.
2 I think _____ is an easy language.
3 I've got friends from _____.
4 My family like _____ food.
5 My teacher speaks _____.
6 At my school we study _____.

1 ★ Complete the table with the words in the box.

~~live~~   doesn't   don't   live   don't   lives

Affirmative
I / You ¹___live___ in London.
He / She ²_____ in Berlin.
We / You / They ³_____ in Paris.

Negative
I / You ⁴_____ speak Spanish.
He / She ⁵_____ speak Mandarin.
We / You / They ⁶_____ speak French.

2 ★★ Complete the text using the correct form of the verbs in brackets.

Language file

Hi! My name's Mohammed. I'm twelve and I'm from Casablanca in Morocco. I _speak_ (speak) three languages – Arabic, French and English. At home, we always ¹_____ (use) Arabic or French – my parents ²_____ (not speak) English. I ³_____ (go) to an international school and we ⁴_____ (speak) French in class. We also ⁵_____ (study) English for four or five hours a week. My teacher, Monsieur Joubert, is very clever – he ⁶_____ (speak) six languages, but he ⁷_____ (not speak) very good Arabic! Sometimes my best friend Yusuf ⁸_____ (use) Arabic in class, but Monsieur Joubert ⁹_____ (not understand)!

3 ★★ Complete the sentences using the correct form of the verbs in the box.

like   use   study   go   ~~do~~   watch   read   play

Irene _____does_____ her homework with a friend.

1 Tom and Emma _____ to a language school on Mondays.
2 Freddie _____ German at school.
3 We _____ English pop music.
4 My grandmother is from Poland and she _____ films in Polish.
5 Olivier and Pascal _____ French books with their father.
6 I _____ a dictionary in my Italian class.
7 He _____ American computer games.

4 ★★★ What do these students do after school every day? Write four affirmative ✓ and four negative ✗ sentences.

	James	Lucy
read books and comics at your home	✓	✗
study Spanish at a language school	✗	✓
play football with friends	✓	✗
go to music lessons	✗	✓
chat on the internet with friends	✓	✓
watch DVDs at home	✗	✗

James _____reads books and comics at home_____.
1 Lucy _____.
2 James _____.
3 Lucy _____.
4 James and Lucy _____.

Lucy ___doesn't read books and comics at home___.
5 James _____.
6 Lucy _____.
7 James _____.
8 James and Lucy _____.

1 ★ Match sentence halves 1–7 with a–g.

1	My dad starts	a lunch at school.
2	I get	b work at 8.00.
3	You have	c TV after school.
4	He finishes	d up at 6.30 in the morning.
5	She watches	e homework in the evening.
6	They do	f to bed before 9.30.
7	I go	g work at five o'clock.

2 ★★ Complete the words in the sentences.

I g <u>e t</u> u <u>p</u> at 7.30.

1 She s _ _ _ _ _
w _ _ _ at the office
at 9.30.

2 They h _ _ _
l _ _ _ _ in a café.

3 He w _ _ _ _ _ _ T _
at home.

4 I d _ m _
h _ _ _ _ _ _ _ in my
bedroom.

5 He g _ _ _ t _
b _ _ at nine o'clock.

3 ★★ Choose the correct answers.

We don't get _____ at 7.00 on Saturdays.

a to (b up) c start d go

1 My teacher _____ work at 7.30.
a starts b goes c gets d watches

2 They _____ TV after dinner.
a have b go c watch d start

3 Karen _____ work at about five o'clock.
a finishes b goes c has d gets

4 You don't _____ to bed at eleven o'clock.
a start b go c watch d finish

5 I always _____ my homework with friends.
a go b have c watch d do

6 She doesn't _____ lunch in a restaurant.
a go b start c have d finish

4 ★★ Dominic is a radio DJ. Complete the sentences about him using the correct form of the verbs in the box. Then put the sentences in the correct order.

start have watch get go finish

a ☐ He _____ work at six o'clock in the morning.

b ☐ He _____ TV in the evening – often a film.

c 1 Dominic _<u>gets</u>_ up at five o'clock.

d ☐ He _____ work after lunch.

e ☐ He _____ to bed at 10.00. He's really tired!

f ☐ He _____ lunch with his friends at 12.30.

5 ★★★ Complete the text.

Clara doesn't go to school. She studies at home with her mother.

I ¹ _<u>get up</u>_ at about seven o'clock. After breakfast it's time for my lessons and we ² _____ work at about nine o'clock. We usually have an English or French lesson. It's always interesting with my mum!

At 1.30 we ³ _____ _____ . I usually have a sandwich. At about 3.00 it's the end of my 'school' day and we ⁴ _____ work. After that I sometimes ⁵ _____ _____ or a DVD for an hour. I love *The Simpsons*! In the evening I ⁶ _____ _____ _____ at the desk in my bedroom. Then I ⁷ _____ _____ _____ at about 9.30.

Present simple: questions

1 ⭐ **Complete the table with the words in the box.**

> do Does ~~Do~~ doesn't don't Do
> don't does do

Questions	Short answers	
	Affirmative	Negative
¹ _Do_ I / you work?	Yes, I / you ² _____.	No, I / you ³ _____.
⁴ _____ he / she / it work?	Yes, he / she / it ⁵ _____.	No, he / she / it ⁶ _____.
⁷ _____ we / you / they work?	Yes, we / you / they ⁸ _____.	No, we / you / they ⁹ _____.

2 ⭐⭐ **Order the words to make questions.**

like / do / you / your / school / new

<u>Do you like your new school?</u>

1 near / the / school / you / live / do

_____

2 you / speak / English / do

_____

3 like / you / do / animals

_____

4 your / friend / does / football / like

_____

5 your / work / parents / do

_____

6 teacher / does / your / use / computer / a / class / in

_____

_____

3 ⭐⭐ **Cheryl Lane is a singer. Write the interview questions.**

(where / you / live?)

<u>Where do you live?</u>

In London and Los Angeles.

1 (you / prefer / London or Los Angeles?)

_____?

I prefer London.

2 (what / your boyfriend / do?)

_____?

He's a footballer.

3 (he / like / your music?)

_____?

Yes, he's a big fan!

4 (how often / you work?)

_____?

Every day.

5 (how / you and your band / travel to concerts?)

_____?

By coach or plane.

6 (when / your friends / come to your concerts?)

_____?

When I play in London.

Adverbs of frequency

4 ⭐⭐ **Write the sentences with the adverb of frequency in the correct position.**

He gets up before 6.00. (always)

<u>He always gets up before 6.00.</u>

1 I go to school on Sundays. (never)

_____

2 Science fiction films are interesting. (usually)

_____

3 We have lunch at our school. (always)

_____

4 You watch films in the evening. (often)

_____

5 My teacher is friendly. (always)

_____

6 She starts work at 8.30. (sometimes)

_____

5 ⭐⭐⭐ **Write the questions. Look at the words in bold to help you choose the correct question word.**

<u>Where do they live?</u>

They live in the **north of England**.

1 _____?

I travel to work **by bus**.

2 _____?

She goes to **Spain** in the summer.

3 _____?

I visit my grandparents **at the weekend**.

4 _____?

They get up at **half past eight**.

5 _____?

He likes **science fiction books**.

6 _____?

I watch TV **every evening**.

READING ■ A cosmopolitan city

1 ★ Read the text. How many nationalities and languages are mentioned? Tick ✓ the correct box.

a ☐ four   b ☐ five   c ☐ six

2 ★★ Read the text again. Match topics 1–4 with paragraphs A–E.

Places to eat   _D_

1 Family   3 A place to visit
2 Different languages   4 Rosa's mother

3 ★★ Read the text again. Complete the sentences.

Rosa is in _Canada_ .

1 Rosa is in Montreal with her _____.
2 She's in Montreal for _____ weeks.
3 People in Montreal speak _____.
4 Rosa's mother doesn't understand some

_____
5 People from _____ live in Montreal.
6 Rosa's favourite place is the _____

_____ .

4 ★★★ Answer the questions. Write complete sentences.

Where does Rosa's aunt live?

She lives in Montreal.

1 How long is Rosa with her aunt?

_____

2 What does Rosa think of Montreal?

_____

3 Is Rosa good at French?

_____

4 What does Rosa's mother do every day?

_____

5 Where does Rosa eat?

_____

6 Why does Rosa like the Mount Royal Park?

_____

Hi, Erin!

A I'm in the Canadian city of Montreal with my mum and dad. It's a fantastic city. My aunt lives here and we're with her for a month.

B Montreal is a very interesting place. It's the biggest bilingual city in the world — a lot of people speak English and French. People speak to me in French in the shops, but when I don't understand they speak in perfect English!

C Mum speaks French fluently. She uses her French every day but she doesn't understand some Canadian French words.

D Montreal is very friendly and there are people from many different countries. We go to Italian cafés in the 'Little Italy' part of the city or to Chinese restaurants in the 'Chinatown' area.

E My favourite place is the Mount Royal Park — it's got an amazing view of the city.

Lots of love,

Rosa

Build your vocabulary

5 ★★ Complete the sentences using the plural form of the words in the box.

> country   person   shop   ~~family~~   word
> class   student   nationality

There are two Italian ___families___ in our road.

1 My father visits a number of _____ for his work — he's in Germany now.
2 How many _____ are on this train? More than 600, I think.
3 London is very cosmopolitan. There are a lot of different _____ in the city.
4 I don't like supermarkets. I prefer small

_____ .

5 At our school we have different _____ for boys and girls.
6 There are a lot of art _____ at the university.
7 Carlos speaks two English _____, 'hello' and 'goodbye'.

Language point: Punctuation

1 ⭐ Rewrite the sentences using capital letters.

my teacher likes british and american films.

<u>My teacher likes British and American films.</u>

1 at school, we speak german and english.
_____

2 there's a great chinese restaurant in toronto.
_____
_____

3 my cousin is from italy and he speaks italian.
_____
_____

4 we study french at our school in ottawa.
_____
_____

5 the pacific ocean is to the west of canada.
_____

6 there are people from asia in quebec.
_____

2 ⭐⭐ Rewrite the sentences using commas, full stops and capital letters.

hugo speaks spanish polish german and french he doesn't speak italian

<u>Hugo speaks Spanish, Polish, German and French.</u>

<u>He doesn't speak Italian.</u>

1 lucy is american she comes from new york
_____

2 i like tennis golf and cycling i don't like football
_____

3 there are students from france italy and china
_____

4 we learn french english german and turkish
_____

5 sharif works in a factory in bangladesh
_____

6 i live in leeds it's a big city in england
_____

⭕ TASK

3 ⭐⭐ Amber is on a German language course in Luxembourg. She has writen a letter to her friend about her class. Look at the notes and complete the letter.

The country:
Luxembourg – tiny
Borders with France, Germany and Belgium
Capital – Luxembourg city

The class:
15 students / 5 different countries
(England, France, Spain, Italy, Turkey)

Languages:
French / English / Spanish / Italian / Turkish

Our German:
me – quite good
my Spanish friend Paula – fantastic

Things for me to learn:
learn more German words
speak German fluently

Language learning ideas:
listen to the radio
read German magazines

Dear Rebecca,

I'm on a German language course in Luxembourg for two weeks. Luxembourg is a ____tiny____ country.
It's got borders with ¹_____.
My language school is in the capital – ²_____.

In my class there are ³_____.
They are from ⁴_____.
The students in my class speak ⁵_____.

My German ⁶_____,
but my Spanish friend Paula speaks ⁷_____.

I want to ⁸_____.

I think it's good to ⁹_____.

See you soon,

Amber xx

4 ⭐⭐⭐ Imagine that you are on an English language course in Edinburgh, the capital of Scotland. Write a letter to a friend about your class and your English.

PROGRESS REVIEW ■ Unit 3

VOCABULARY ■ Countries, nationalities and languages

1   Complete the sentences with a country, nationality or language.

1   Is he from France?
No, but his mother is _____.

2   My friends Naomi and Kenji are from Japan. They're _____.

3   Where are the cities of New York and Miami? They're in _____.

4   My father is from Poland. He speaks _____.

5   I love big pizzas. _____ food is my favourite!

6   Ottawa, Toronto and Vancouver are cities in _____.

7   She lives in _____, but she doesn't speak Spanish.

8   Do you like music from Brazil?
Yes, I do. I love _____ music.

9   We're German and we're from Berlin. It's the capital of _____.

10 Sydney is an Australian city. It's in the south of _____.

> **I can talk about countries, nationalities and languages.**
>
> MY EVALUATION ◻◻◻◻

READING ■ A cosmopolitan city

2   Complete the sentences using the plural form of one of the words in brackets.

1   My favourite English _____ are amazing and incredible! (nationality / word)

2   There are hundreds of _____ in this shopping centre. (shop / class)

3   Are there a lot of _____ in the library today? Yes, it's quite noisy. (country / person)

4   Do you like your English _____? (nationality / class)

5   Children speak different languages at my school. There are a lot of different _____. (country / nationality)

6   Two _____ at my school are from Germany. (student / class)

7   What are your favourite _____? France and Spain. (country / shop)

8   There are some Brazilian _____ in those new flats. (family / word)

> **I can understand an article about people living in London.**
>
> MY EVALUATION ◻◻◻◻

LANGUAGE FOCUS ■ Present simple: affirmative and negative

3   Write sentences using the present simple affirmative and negative.

1   my mother / go to work / at 10.00
_____
_____

2   we / not learn Spanish / at school
_____
_____

3   I / watch a film / every weekend
_____
_____

4   he / not live / in a big city
_____
_____

5   she / study / Japanese and German
_____
_____

6   they / not like / Chinese food
_____
_____

> **I can use the present simple to talk about facts and routines.**
>
> MY EVALUATION ◻◻◻◻

VOCABULARY AND LISTENING ■ Routines

4 Sara works for a magazine and she studies Italian at a language school. Complete the sentences about her.

1 I g_____ u_____ at seven o'clock. It's early for me!
2 I s_____ w_____ at the office at about half past nine.
3 I h_____ l_____ at 2.00. I often have soup.
4 I f_____ w_____ at five o'clock. It's time to go home!
5 I d_____ m_____ h_____ in my room at about 7.30.
6 At 9.00 I w_____ T_____ or listen to music.
7 At 11.00 I g_____ t_____ b_____.

> **I can talk about daily routines.**
> MY EVALUATION ☐☐☐☐

LANGUAGE FOCUS ■ Present simple: questions

5 Complete the dialogues.

1 _____
(you / live) near here?
Yes, I do. I live in those flats.
2 Where _____
(your father / work)?
In a factory not far from here.
3 What _____
(you and your friends / do) at the weekend?
We go to the sports centre in town.
4 How often _____
(your best friend / visit) you?
Every day. She's very popular with my family!
5 _____
(your best friend / like) hip hop music?
Yes, she does. She loves modern music.
6 What time _____
(you / go) to school?
About 8.00, but I'm usually late!

> **I can ask people about their routines and habits.**
> MY EVALUATION ☐☐☐☐

SPEAKING ■ Talking about likes and dislikes

6 Complete the dialogue with the words in the box.

> playing about mind hate do really watching

Robbie What ¹_____ you like doing?
Joe I really enjoy ²_____ tennis with my dad. He's fantastic! What ³_____ you?
Robbie I ⁴_____ doing sport! It's boring! I like ⁵_____ black and white films on TV with my friends.
Joe But they're ⁶_____ bad! I don't ⁷_____ listening to classical music, but I hate old films!

> **I can talk about things I like and don't like doing.**
> MY EVALUATION ☐☐☐☐

WRITING ■ Country and language report

7 Choose the correct answers.

1 Mexico has got a border _____ the USA.
a of b with c for d up
2 The Pacific Ocean is _____ the west of Mexico.
a to b from c in d of
3 _____ Mexicans speak Spanish.
a More b A lot c Most d Less
4 Spanish is the _____ language in Mexico City.
a main b currency c area d office
5 But _____ from other countries live in Mexico city too.
a population b people c persons d nations
6 In _____, there are people from Guatemala and Venezuela in Mexico.
a most b mostly c particularly d particular

> **I can write a report about a country.**
> MY EVALUATION ☐☐☐☐

4 ⬜⬜⬜⬜⬜⬜⬜⬜⬜ The wild side

VOCABULARY ● Animals

1 ⭐ Label the photos with nine of the words in the box.

> snake   frog   elephant   bear   parrot
> ~~owl~~   shark   crocodile   whale   spider
> seal   butterfly   falcon   chameleon
> fly   human

owl

1 _____

2 _____   3 _____

4 _____   5 _____

6 _____   7 _____

8 _____   9 _____

2 ⭐⭐ Do the *Animal quiz*.

> ## Animal quiz: Who am I?
>
> I've got a big nose, I live for up to seventy years and I'm 6,000 kilos. _____elephant_____
>
> 1 I'm blue, green and yellow, I live in Brazil and I fly. _____
>
> 2 I've got four small legs and a very big mouth. I eat animals. _____
>
> 3 I live for seventy years. I swim in the sea. I'm 136,000 kilos. _____
>
> 4 I'm different colours. I like flowers. I fly but I'm not a bird. _____
>
> 5 I've got big eyes. I'm grey or brown and I eat seven kilos of fish every day.
>
> _____
>
> 6 I eat insects. I've got eight legs.
>
> _____

3 ⭐⭐ Complete the table with the words in the box. Use some of the words twice.

> elephant   butterfly   crocodile   falcon
> human   owl   ~~parrot~~   shark   seal
> whale   bear

fly	parrot
swim	
two legs	
four legs	

4 ⭐⭐⭐ Write affirmative and negative sentences about six of the animals in exercise 3.

<u>A parrot doesn't swim. It's got two legs.</u>

1 _____

2 _____

3 _____

4 _____

5 _____

6 _____

1 ★ Complete the table with the words in the box

~~am~~ are am not aren't is isn't

Affirmative	
I ¹ _am_ He / She / It ² _____ You / We / You / They ³ _____	studying.
Negative	
I ⁴ _____ He / She / It ⁵ _____ You / We / You / They ⁶ _____	reading.

2 ★★ Complete the sentences using the *-ing* form of the verbs in brackets.

She _____'s living_____ (live) with her grandparents at the moment.

1 Jacob _____ (watch) TV.
2 Mum and dad _____ (fly) to Spain.
3 Your cat _____ (sit) on my bed!
4 Dad _____ (practise) the guitar.
5 We _____ (run) in the park.
6 The bus _____ (stop) near the shops.

3 ★★ What are they doing? Write sentences using the phrases in the box in the present continuous.

play basketball   write an email   go to bed
swim   ~~make dinner~~   watch a film
do an exam

Clara is in the kitchen.
She's making dinner.

1 Rachel is at the computer.
_____

2 Daniel and Max are at the sports centre.
_____

3 Zak is in the classroom.
_____

4 Callum is in his bedroom.
_____

5 Samuel and Anna are at the cinema.
_____

6 The dog is in the river.
_____

4 ★★ Write affirmative ✓ or negative ✗ sentences.

he / watch / a programme about bears ✗
He isn't watching a programme about bears.

1 they / listen / to music ✗
_____

2 we / eat / dinner at home ✓
_____

3 she / play / tennis in the park ✓
_____

4 we / study / snakes at school ✗
_____

5 you / write / an email in English ✗
_____
_____

6 they / visit / some friends ✓
_____

7 he / look / at the teacher ✗
_____

5 ★★★ Write affirmative and negative sentences about the picture. Use the present continuous.

Dan   Amy   Tom   Sara   Pat   Ross and Jack   Ruby and Sue

Pat is talking to the teacher.
Dan isn't sleeping.

1 _____
2 _____
3 _____
4 _____
5 _____
6 _____
7 _____
8 _____

VOCABULARY ■ Verbs: animal behaviour

1 ★ Find eleven more verbs.

P	R	O	T	E	C	T	H	Z	R	Y	H
N	F	H	I	D	E	Q	V	K	O	B	W
H	E	X	W	C	H	A	S	E	E	U	P
U	E	J	R	G	A	X	V	Y	Q	T	L
N	D	C	A	T	C	H	D	F	U	L	A
T	Q	B	K	C	T	J	V	I	C	E	Y
G	K	U	D	E	A	T	R	G	L	Z	W
D	Y	I	Y	X	N	W	E	H	K	R	I
I	V	L	Q	H	E	L	P	T	G	Y	T
G	Z	D	B	S	Q	D	S	K	V	C	H

2 ★★ Match definitions 1–7 with words a–g.

1 When an animal gives food to its babies.
2 When people run after an animal and kill it for food or sport.
3 When an animal makes a house or something new.
4 When two animals are angry they do this.
5 When an animal makes a big hole.
6 When people do something good and make an animal's life easier.
7 When an animal puts food in its mouth.

a build
b feed
c fight
d hunt
e eat
f dig
g help

3 ★★ Complete the text with the words in the box.

> feed   hide   ~~chase~~   eat   catch   dig
> protect

Black bears

American black bears aren't dangerous and they don't usually ___chase___ or attack people. Bears are quiet animals. When they see people they sometimes ¹_____ in trees.

Bears ²_____ a lot every day – especially insects. They often ³_____ holes and look for them.

Bears also like the water; they sometimes swim in rivers and ⁴_____ fish in their big mouths.

Black bears have babies every two years. The mothers ⁵_____ the babies on milk and later on insects.

Pollution and construction are changing the habitats of the black bear. They're now in danger. It's important to ⁶_____ them.

4 ★★★ Write sentences about the animals in the photos using the present continuous affirmative and negative.

The spider is catching the fly. It isn't protecting
the fly.

1 _____
_____

2 _____
_____

3 _____
_____

Present continuous: questions

1 ★ Complete the table with the words in the box.

> aren't am is ~~Am~~ 'm not Are isn't
> are Is

Questions	Short answers
¹ _Am_ I listening?	Yes, I ² _____. No, I ³ _____.
⁴ _____ he / she / it listening?	Yes, he / she / it ⁵ _____. No, he / she / it ⁶ _____.
⁷ _____ we / you / they listening?	Yes, we / you / they ⁸ _____. No, we / you / they ⁹ _____.

2 ★★ Order the words to make questions. Then match them with answers a–g.

speaking / who / she / is / to

Who is she speaking to? _____ c

1 going / you / where / are

_____ __

2 is / what / he / doing

_____ __

3 are / listening / what / they / to

_____ __

4 studying / she / is / what

_____ __

5 writing / to / who / you / are

_____ __

6 they / eating / are / what

_____ __

a To the train station.   e Playing tennis.
b My friend Paula.   f Bread and cheese.
c Her mother.   g French and German.
d English pop songs.

Present continuous and present simple

3 ★★ Complete the sentences with the words in the box.

> are watching ~~study~~ isn't working
> plays 's playing doesn't work watch

At my school I ____study____ French and Spanish.

1 Mark is at the park now. He _____ football.

2 Cara and Rosa _____ TV for hours every day.

3 My dad _____ at the factory today. He's on holiday.

4 Where are Ben and Sam? They _____ a film about animals.

5 Maria is into sport. She _____ basketball every week.

6 My mum is a doctor. She _____ in an office.

4 ★★ Complete the letter with the present simple or present continuous form of the verbs in brackets.

Hi Anna

I'm on holiday in Kenya. We usually ____go____ (go) on holiday to Scotland every year but this year we ¹_____ (do) a safari in the Maasai Mara national park in Kenya!

It's really interesting here. Every day we ²_____ (drive) around the park and we ³_____ (see) a lot of different animals. My dad always ⁴_____ (take) a lot of photos of them.

I ⁵_____ (look) out of my window now. There are a lot of elephants and they ⁶_____ (eat) the trees near our hotel.

See you soon.

Robbie

5 ★★★ Write affirmative or negative sentences that are true for you. Use the present simple or the present continuous.

> at the moment every day usually
> now never not usually

I make my breakfast every day.
I'm not writing an email at the moment.

1 _____

2 _____

3 _____

4 _____

5 _____

6 _____

The Secret Life of Honey Bees

A Bees are very important to us. They are the only insects that give us food: honey. We see them every day in spring and summer, but what do you know about them?

B Bees live in hives. There are often 40,000–45,000 bees in one hive! Hives are hot places with a temperature of about 33°C.

C There are two types of bee in a hive: the queen bee and the worker bees. There is only one queen bee, and she is very important. She lives for about three years. The worker bees live for four to six weeks. They usually fly about two kilometres a day to look for flowers, but they sometimes fly up to fourteen kilometres!

D A lot of bee colonies are disappearing at the moment in North America and in some European countries. We don't understand why, but some people think that pollution is a problem for the bees.

1 ⭐ **Read the text. Tick ✓ the correct box.**

The text is about …

a ☐ the life of honey bees in very hot countries.

b ☐ honey bees in American and European cities.

c ☐ honey bees and the different things they do.

2 ⭐⭐ **Match topics 1–3 with paragraphs A–D.**

Types of bee _____C_____

1 Bees in danger _____
2 Where bees live _____
3 Introduction _____

3 ⭐⭐ **Read the text again. Are the sentences *true* or *false*?**

A lot of different insects give us food. _false_

1 Hives are cold places. _____
2 Two different types of bees live in a hive. _____
3 Worker bees live for three years. _____
4 Bees sometimes fly fourteen kilometres. _____
5 Bees are dying in Australia and Japan. _____
6 People don't understand why bee colonies are disappearing. _____

4 ⭐⭐⭐ **Answer the questions. Write complete sentences.**

Where do honey bees live?
They live in hives.

1 How many bees are there in a hive?
_____

2 What is the name of the important bee in a hive?
_____

3 How long do worker bees live for?
_____

4 How many kilometres do bees usually fly?
_____

5 Where are bee colonies disappearing?
_____

6 What is a problem for bees?
_____

Build your vocabulary

5 ⭐⭐ **Complete the dialogues with the words in the box.**

> save   accidents   pollution   actions
> approximately   ~~attack~~

Do black bears ____attack____ people?
Not usually.

1 How many tigers are there in India?
_____ 1,500.

2 Is the air clean in your city?
No, there's a lot of _____.

3 Is it important to _____ whales?
Yes. Some types of whales are becoming extinct.

4 How many people have car _____ every year?
Quite a lot, I think.

5 Do people need to change their _____?
Yes, definitely.

Language point: *because*

1 ★ Choose the correct words.

He studies the climate (**because**) / **or** he's interested in polar bears.

1 Ben has got a camera **because** / **but** he doesn't take a lot of photos.
2 It's important to protect elephants **because** / **and** they're in danger.
3 Bears sometimes catch fish in rivers **because** / **or** lakes.
4 Whales are in danger **because** / **and** there's a lot of pollution in the sea.
5 Falcons eat animals **because** / **but** they don't usually eat fruit.
6 The seals are swimming to the beach **and** / **because** there's a shark in the sea.

2 ★★ Match 1–4 with a–d and write sentences with *because.*

1 My grandmother likes my dogs   a he's into taekwondo.
2 Antonio goes to Italian restaurants   b they're very friendly.
3 Hector has got a book about martial arts   c he likes pizzas.
4 Megan is interested in maths   d she's got a good teacher.

1 <u>My grandmother likes my dogs because</u>
   <u>they're very friendly.</u>

2 _____
  _____

3 _____
  _____

4 _____
  _____

○ TASK

3 ★★ Read the notes about Ali Kazan. Then use the notes to complete the text.

Name: Ali Kazan
Age: 46
Job: zoo assistant
Place of work: Drusilla's family zoo
                  near Eastbourne, UK
When: Monday – Friday
Get up: early
Start: six o'clock
Jobs: clean the parrot cages / help in the café / chat to visitors
Lunch: in the café
Now: give food to the elephants 'It's fun.'

Ali Kazan is __46 years old__. He's a ¹_____.

He works at ²_____ in the
³_____. Ali works at the zoo from
⁴_____. He ⁵_____ because
he starts work ⁶_____. Every day he
⁷_____. He has lunch ⁸_____.

At the moment, ⁹_____. He thinks this
job ¹⁰_____. He says, 'I really like the
elephants because they're always friendly!'

4 ★★★ Choose one of the jobs in the box and write a short text. Use the text in exercise 3 to help you.

vet   wildlife photographer
pet shop owner

MY EVALUATION   Check your progress. Do the exercises and then complete your own evaluation.

⬤◻◻◻ I need to try this again. ⬤⬤⬤◻ I am happy with this.

⬤⬤◻◻ I could do this better. ⬤⬤⬤⬤ I can do this very well.

VOCABULARY ■ Animals

1 Complete the words in the sentences.

1 A w _ _ _ _ is a big animal. It lives in the sea.

2 How many legs has a s _ _ _ _ _ got? Eight.

3 A c _ _ _ _ _ _ _ _ is amazing – it changes colour!

4 An o _ _ hunts small animals. It flies in the sky.

5 A s _ _ _ _ hasn't got any legs. Sometimes it's dangerous.

6 What is big and grey with a long nose? An e _ _ _ _ _ _ _.

7 My p _ _ _ _ _ is a clever bird. It says 'hello'.

8 There's a beautiful red and yellow b _ _ _ _ _ _ _ _ on that flower.

> **I can describe animals.**
> MY EVALUATION ◻◻◻◻

READING ■ The red list

2 Complete the questions with the words in the box.

> actions   pollution   approximately
> protect   attack   accidents

1 Does this factory make a lot of _____?

2 Do crocodiles _____ and kill people?

3 Are people's _____ a problem for animals?

4 Are there a lot of bad _____ on the roads here?

5 Do you want to help _____ tigers?

6 Are there _____ thirty students in every class in this school?

> **I can understand an article about animals in danger.**
> MY EVALUATION ◻◻◻◻

LANGUAGE FOCUS ■ Present continuous: affirmative and negative

3 Write sentences using the present continuous.

1 we / watch / a DVD about animals

_____

2 they / not protect / tigers

_____

3 I / feed / my two dogs

_____

4 the bear / hunt / in the mountains

_____

5 she / not swim / in the river

_____

6 I / not hide / in the tree

> **I can talk about things happening now.**
> MY EVALUATION ◻◻◻◻

VOCABULARY AND LISTENING ■ Verbs: animal behaviour

4 Choose the correct answers.

1 That rabbit is _____ a big hole.
   a building   b digging   c chasing   d hunting

2 The falcon is _____ its babies with insects.
   a protecting   b eating   c feeding   d chasing

3 The bear wants to eat. It's _____ that rabbit.
   a hunting   b playing with
   c protecting   d feeding

4 Those animals are _____ a new home.
   a eating   b chasing   c helping   d building

5 The frog is hungry. It's _____ some food.
   a fighting   b building   c eating   d feeding

> **I can understand an interview about animal behaviour.**
> MY EVALUATION ◻◻◻◻

LANGUAGE FOCUS ● Present continuous questions

5 Complete the questions and short answers.

1 _____ he _____ (get up) now?
No, he _____.

2 _____ they _____ (watch) a film about sharks ?
Yes, they _____.

3 _____ we _____ (have) lunch?
Yes, we _____.

4 _____ she _____ (talk) about endangered animals?
Yes, she _____.

5 _____ you _____ (use) that dictionary?
No, I _____.

6 _____ it _____ (eat) the food?
Yes, it _____.

7 _____ the seals _____ (swim) in the sea?
Yes, they _____.

8 _____ the bear _____ (hunt) for food?
No, it _____.

> **I can ask people about their routines and what they are doing now.**
>
> MY EVALUATION ☐☐☐☐

SPEAKING ● Phoning a friend

6 Order the sentences to make a dialogue.

a ☐ **Clara** Fine, thanks. Listen, what are you doing at the moment?

b ☐ **Clara** OK, great! Give me a call. Bye!

c ☐ **Alex** Yes, it's an interesting match. We can meet later if you want.

d ☐ **Clara** Hi, Alex. It's Clara.

e ☐ **Alex** I'm playing tennis in the park.

f ☐ **Alex** Hello, Clara. How are you?

g ☐ **Clara** Are you having a good time?

> **I can talk about what I'm doing now.**
>
> MY EVALUATION ☐☐☐☐

WRITING ● A description of a wildlife photo

7 Complete the text with the words in the box.

> standing extinct because called
> photo live protect chasing

The animal in this ¹_____ is a Sumatran tiger. Here it's ²_____ near some trees. Maybe it's hunting or ³_____ a small animal.

Sumatran tigers ⁴_____ on the small island of Sumatra in Indonesia. They sometimes swim and they like eating fish! Females have two or three babies, ⁵_____ cubs, every three years.

Sumatran tigers are on the 'red list' ⁶_____ they are in danger of becoming ⁷_____. There are only 400 of these tigers now on Sumatra. I think it's important to ⁸_____ these animals.

> **I can write an article about an animal.**
>
> MY EVALUATION ☐☐☐☐

VOCABULARY ▪ Activities in and out of school

1 ⭐ Match sentences 1–6 with pictures a–f.

1 I've got a science class today.
2 And I've got a maths exam!
3 But I've also got art. It's my favourite.
4 And drama too. I love it!
5 After school I've got French homework.
6 And this evening I've got a football match.

 a ⬜

 b ⬜

 c ⬜

 d ⬜

 e ⬜

 f ⬜

2 ⭐⭐ Choose the correct answers.

I love studying _____, especially drawing.
(a art) **b** drama **c** basketball **d** chess

1 She's interested in _____ because she's good with numbers.
a PE **b** music **c** maths **d** history

2 He plays _____ and he's in the school team.
a drama **b** football **c** PE **d** geography

3 There are questions about Julius Caesar and Napoleon in the _____ exam.
a history **b** chess **c** dance **d** science

4 I like learning things about computers in _____.
a football **b** drama **c** PE **d** ICT

5 We often sing in our _____ classes.
a art **b** music **c** geography **d** chess

6 She loves learning _____ in her language class.
a French **b** drama **c** music **d** maths

3 ⭐⭐ Complete the sentences with the words in the box.

> match   practice   homework   ~~class~~
> exam   football   English

Susan is listening to the teacher in her French _____class_____.

1 Sam is revising for a geography _____.
2 Tom plays in a _____ match every Saturday.
3 Julia has got dance _____ after school.
4 Tom has got a lot of _____ homework.
5 Suzy's class are watching a tennis _____.
6 We've always got loads of science _____.

4 ⭐⭐⭐ Write eight sentences about activities in and out of school.

I really like history classes.

1 I don't mind _____.
2 I hate _____.
3 I don't like _____.
4 I like _____ once a week.
5 _____ classes.
6 _____ practice on Friday mornings.
7 _____ matches.
8 _____ homework every day.

can for ability and permission

1 ⭐ Complete the table with the words in the box.

> can't   ~~can~~   Can   can't   can   swim

Affirmative
I / You / He / She / It / We / You / They ¹ __can__ swim.

Negative
I / You / He / She / It / We / You / They ² _____ swim.

Questions
³ _____ I / you / he / she / it / we / you / they ⁴ _____ ?

Short answers	
Affirmative	**Negative**
Yes, I / you / he / she / it / we / you / they ⁵ _____.	No, I / you / he / she / it / we / you / they ⁶ _____.

2 ⭐⭐ What are the people saying? Write sentences with *can*, *can't* or *Can ...?*

I / say / 'hello' in Spanish.

I can say 'hello' in Spanish.

1 I / not swim / !

_____

2 she / use / your laptop / ?

_____

3 you / not go / to Jack's house

_____

4 she / eat / some food now

_____

5 we / wear / these clothes to school / ?

_____

3 ⭐⭐ Write sentences with *can* or *can't* and the words in the box. Then write P (permission) or A (ability) next to each sentence.

> wear   play   use   ~~run~~   watch   buy
> go   speak   read   dance

That's James. He __can run__ very fast. __A__

1 She _____ Italian and Japanese. She's very good at languages. _____

2 _____ I _____ that film on TV? _____

3 My grandparents _____ a computer but they want to learn. _____

4 I'm sorry. You _____ to the cinema now. _____

5 He loves music and he _____ the guitar. _____

6 You _____ that T-shirt to school if you want. _____

7 _____ you _____ the tango? _____

8 My baby sister _____ or write. _____

9 _____ I _____ a new mobile phone in that shop? _____

4 ⭐⭐⭐ Write eight questions or sentences with *can* or *can't* for permission or ability. Use the ideas in the box.

Permission
go to bed at ... buy a ... go to ... watch ... play with ... use ... phone ...

Ability
speak ... play ... (sport) play the ... (instrument) swim ... (metres) run ... (metres)

Can I go to bed at eleven o'clock?

My sister can play the guitar.

1 _____

2 _____

3 _____

4 _____

5 _____

6 _____

7 _____

8 _____

VOCABULARY ◾ Food and drink

1 ⭐ **Choose the word that doesn't match.**

cheese   egg   (pasta)

1 fizzy drinks
juice   sweets

2 fish   vegetables
salad

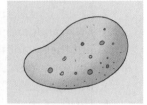

3 crisps   chips   cheese

4 pasta   burger   rice

5 ice cream   meat
fish

2 ⭐⭐ **Complete the lists with the words in the box.**

> burgers   chips   crisps   fish   fizzy drinks
> ice cream   beans   nuts   water   salad
> sweets   ~~apple~~

Very healthy!		Not very healthy!	
apple		_____	
_____		_____	
_____		_____	
_____		_____	
_____		_____	
_____		_____	

3 ⭐⭐ **Complete the crossword.**

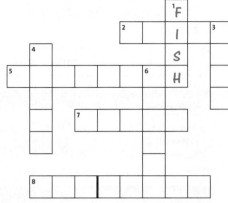

DOWN
1 It swims in the sea and you can eat it.
3 A hot food. You eat it with a spoon.
4 This popular food comes from Italy.
6 It's yellow and comes from milk.

ACROSS
2 You make them from potatoes.
5 Bread with meat, cheese or salad in it.
7 This is a very healthy drink.
8 It's cold and very popular in summer.

4 ⭐⭐ **Choose the correct answers.**

Quiz ## Food around the world

The Italians make very good _____.
(a ice cream)   **b** crisps   **c** chips   **d** soup

1 In the UK people eat fish and _____.
   a beans   **b** crisps   **c** chips   **d** nuts
2 In Japan there is a lot of food with _____.
   a apples   **b** cheese   **c** eggs   **d** rice
3 An average American eats more than 100
   _____ a year.
   a nuts   **b** burgers   **c** crisps   **d** chips
4 In France people make _____ called
   Camembert, Brie and Roquefort.
   a cheese   **b** soup   **c** ice cream   **d** bread
5 The world's most popular _____ is cola.
   a soup   **b** juice   **c** fizzy drink   **d** water
6 Perrier and Vichy are the names of _____
   from France.
   a water   **b** pasta   **c** meat   **d** fish

5 ⭐⭐⭐ **Write a word group for fruit or vegetables. Put in ten or more words.**

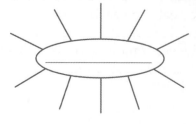

1 ★ Look at the table. Choose the correct words.

	Uncountable	Countable
Affirmative	There's ¹a lot of / any rice.	There are ²much / a lot of apples.
	There's ³many / some pasta.	There are ⁴some / any sweets.
Negative	There isn't ⁵much / many cheese.	There aren't ⁶much / many crisps.
	There isn't ⁷any / many water.	There aren't ⁸much / any eggs.

2 ★ Write C (countable) or U (uncountable).

apple   _C_

1 bean   _____
2 cheese   _____
3 chip   _____
4 egg   _____
5 milk   _____
6 nut   _____
7 pasta   _____
8 soup   _____
9 sandwich   _____
10 water   _____

3 ★★ Look at the table and write sentences about Carl's diet. Use *some, any, much, many* and *a lot of*.

Breakfast	✗
Lunch	sandwiches ✓✓ crisps ✓✓✓ fruit ✗
Dinner	pasta ✓ meat ✓✓✓ vegetables ✓
10.00	ice cream ✓✓

Carl eats ___*some*___ sandwiches for lunch.

He doesn't eat ___*much*___ pasta for dinner.

1 Carl doesn't eat _____ food for breakfast.
2 For lunch he usually eats _____ crisps.
3 But he doesn't eat _____ fruit.
4 For dinner he doesn't eat _____ vegetables.
5 But he eats _____ meat.
6 At 10.00 he often eats _____ ice cream.

4 ★★★ Write affirmative and negative sentences about what you eat or drink in these situations. Use *some, any, much, many* and *a lot of*.

At home **I drink a lot of juice.**

At school **we don't eat any sweets.**

1 At home _____
_____ .
2 At school _____
_____ .
3 On my birthday _____
_____ .
4 On holiday _____
_____ .
5 In the winter _____
_____ .
6 In the summer _____
_____ .
7 On a picnic _____
_____ .

5 ★★ Complete the sentences with *a, an* or *the*.

Do you go to __*the*__ Italian café next to the school?

1 I always have _____ sandwich for my lunch.
2 Do you like _____ food at your school? Yes, I do.
3 I've got _____ apple and some crisps. _____ apple is nice and red.
4 He sometimes buys _____ pizza at the weekend.
5 Do you like _____ pasta in that restaurant?
6 Where's _____ school canteen? It's over there.
7 She often has _____ fizzy drink in the park.
8 I've got two sandwiches for us. Do you want the cheese sandwich or _____ meat sandwich?
9 It's hot today. Would you like _____ ice cream?
10 He's eating _____ burger and chips for lunch, and _____ burger is very hot.

A DAY AT SUMMERHILL

Summerhill is a boarding school in south-east England. It's a school with a difference because the teachers don't make the rules – the students make them.

Breakfast is from 8.00 until 9.00 and lessons start at 9.30. Holly is a student here – she likes lessons. She's studying a lot of subjects. Ivan is a student here, too. He isn't interested in lessons and he can play all day if he wants.

At 12.30 it's lunchtime, and the students and teachers eat together. There are three choices of meal: one with meat, a vegetarian option and a salad bar, too.

At 1.45 there's a meeting. The students and teachers talk about problems and they can change school rules in this meeting. Then there are free-time activities: orchestra practice, drama group or sport.

Ivan goes shopping in town. Holly plays the violin with the orchestra.

At 5.30 it's dinner time. After dinner students chat and do homework. Younger children go to bed before 9.30, but older children can go to bed when they want.

So that's a day at Summerhill. Do you think school is better when the students make the rules?

1 ⭐ Read the text. Tick ✓ the correct box.

The text is about …

a ☐ a school for adults.

b ☐ a boarding school for adults and children.

c ☐ a boarding school for children.

2 ⭐⭐ Read the text again. Match sentence halves 1–6 with a–f.

1 Summerhill is   a everyone has dinner.

2 Breakfast is   b is interested in lessons.

3 Holly   c a school with a difference.

4 Ivan   d at 8.00 a.m.

5 There's   e wants to play.

6 At 5.30   f vegetarian food.

3 ⭐⭐ Read the text again. Choose the correct answers.

Lessons at Summerhill start after _____.

ⓐ breakfast   b lunch   c dinner

1 The lessons begin at _____.
   a 8.00   b 9.00   c 9.30

2 Ivan doesn't like _____.
   a shopping   b doing lessons
   c playing the violin

3 Holly is studying _____ subjects.
   a a lot of   b one   c two or three

4 At lunchtime the students eat with _____.
   a the very young students   b the teachers
   c the sports teachers

4 ⭐⭐⭐ Answer the questions. Write complete sentences.

Where is Summerhill?

It's in south-east England.

1 What is unusual about Summerhill?

_____

2 When do the students and teachers discuss problems?

_____

3 What can the students have for lunch?

_____

4 What do students do in the afternoon?

_____

5 What do you think about Summerhill?

_____

Build your vocabulary

5 ⭐⭐ Complete the sentences using the correct form of the words in the box.

> be homesick   share a room   have a break
> chat with friends   be busy   ~~work abroad~~

1 When I'm older I want to _work abroad_ .

2 I often _____ on the phone.

3 I _____ with my sister.

4 She hates boarding school. She _____.

5 We finish lessons at 11.00 and _____.

6 Do you want to come to drama club?
No, sorry. I _____.

Language point: Giving examples

1 ⭐ Rewrite the sentences with the phrases in brackets.

Suzy has got a lot of hobbies reading, art and photography. (such as)

Suzy has got a lot of hobbies, such as reading, art and photography.

1 There are clubs after school drama, music and sport. (for example)

_____

_____

2 I'm into pop singers Kylie, Mika and Duffy. (like)

_____

_____

3 Dan is into sports cycling and tennis. (such as)

_____

_____

4 Are you interested in film stars Matt Damon and Orlando Bloom? (like)

_____

_____

2 ⭐⭐ Join the sentences to make one sentence. Use the phrases in brackets.

I like fruit. I eat apples and bananas. (for example)

I like fruit, for example apples and bananas.

1 She enjoys team sports. She enjoys football and basketball. (like)

_____

_____

2 My dad travels to different countries. He goes to Poland, Germany and Turkey. (such as)

_____

_____

3 I've got a lot of things in my bag. There's a pen, a notebook and a dictionary. (for example)

_____

_____

4 I put different things on my pizzas. I use cheese, meat or vegetables. (such as)

_____

_____

○ TASK

3 ⭐⭐ Adam is visiting a school in Germany. Read about the school and complete Adam's email.

A German school

7.30:	lessons start
7.30 – 1.30:	six lessons, 45 minutes
Compulsory subjects:	German, maths, English, science
Optional subjects:	art, music, history
Lunch:	at home, meat with vegetables / pasta
After-school clubs:	drama, music, sport, etc.

● ● ●

Delete	Reply	Reply All	Forward	New	Mailboxes	Get Mail	Q▾ From

I'm visiting a school in Germany for two weeks. Lessons ___ **start at** ___ 7.30. There are six ¹_____ every day and the lessons ²_____. There are a lot of ³_____ subjects, ⁴_____ German and ⁵_____. You can choose other subjects, for example ⁶_____. School finishes ⁷_____ and students eat ⁸_____ at home. There ⁹_____ after school, such as ¹⁰_____.

4 ⭐⭐⭐ Describe your perfect school. Use the text in exercise 3 to help you.

MY EVALUATION Check your progress. Do the exercises and then complete your own evaluation.

⬛⬜⬜⬜ I need to try this again.   ⬛⬛⬛⬜ I am happy with this.

⬛⬛⬜⬜ I could do this better.   ⬛⬛⬛⬛ I can do this very well.

VOCABULARY ● Activities in and out of school

1 Complete the sentences with the words in the box.

> maths basketball ICT dance science
> French geography PE

1 I like learning about different countries. _____ is my favourite subject.
2 Are you doing football in _____ at school?
No, we're doing tennis and _____ .
3 In my languages classes I'm studying English and _____ .
4 She always learns new things about computers in _____ .
5 What is 356 + 598?
Ask Alex – he's good at _____ .
6 We're studying the human eye in _____ .
7 I want to learn the tango at the after-school _____ club.

> **I can talk about my school timetable and after-school activities.**
> MY EVALUATION ⬜⬜⬜⬜

READING ● Boarding school

2 Complete the dialogues at a boarding school with the words in the box. Use the correct form of the verbs.

> share a room chat with friends be busy
> be homesick work abroad have a break

1 Why are you unhappy, Anna?
Because I _____ and I want to see my mum.
2 Do you _____ with Emily?
No, with Lily and Kate.

3 Can I talk to you now, Mrs Smith?
No, sorry I _____ with some work.
4 What does your dad do?
He _____ – he's in Japan now.
5 What do you do in the evening?
I _____ – we usually talk about films.
6 This homework is boring!
Yes, I want to stop and _____ .

> **I can understand an interview about boarding school life.**
> MY EVALUATION ⬜⬜⬜⬜

LANGUAGE FOCUS ● *can* for ability and permission

3 Rewrite the sentences. Use affirmative (✓), negative (✗) or question (?) forms. Then write P (permission) or A (ability) next to each sentence.

1 Can he listen to the CD? ✗
_____
2 Can they run 100 metres in 10 seconds? ✓
_____
3 I can watch TV. (?)
_____
4 You can't speak Spanish. ✓
_____
5 We can't go to the park now. (?)
_____
6 She can play the piano. ✗
_____
7 He can swim fast (?)
_____
8 Can we go to the cinema? ✓
_____

> **I can talk about things we can and can't do.**
> MY EVALUATION ⬜⬜⬜⬜

VOCABULARY AND LISTENING ■ Food and drink

4 Complete the words in the sentences.

1 Do you like fizzy drinks? No, I prefer w _ _ _ _ – it's healthier for you.

2 I have some fruit every day. Usually an a _ _ _ _ and a pear.

3 Is there any m _ _ _ in that sandwich? Yes, there's some chicken.

4 People often eat r _ _ _ with Chinese food.

5 Do you want a drink? Yes, orange j _ _ _ _, please.

6 It's very hot today. I think it's time for an i _ _ c _ _ _ _!

7 In Italian restaurants you can eat pizzas and p _ _ _ _.

8 I want to make a sandwich but I haven't got any b _ _ _ _.

> **I can talk about my eating habits.**
>
> MY EVALUATION ☐☐☐☐

LANGUAGE FOCUS ■ Countable and uncountable nouns: *a / an, the, some, any, much, many,* and *a lot of*

5 Complete the sentences with one of the words in brackets.

1 Richard eats _____ crisps. (any / much / a lot of)

2 There aren't _____ apples on that old tree. (some / many / much)

3 I've got _____ nice sweets. (some / any / much)

4 Here you are. There isn't _____ soup but you can have some bread. (much / many / some)

5 Oh no! We haven't got _____ cheese for the pizza. (many / any / some)

6 It's good to eat _____ vegetables. (many / much / a lot of)

7 Do you usually eat in _____ canteen at school? (a / an / the)

8 Have you got _____ sandwich for lunch today? (a / an / the)

> **I can talk about food and meals.**
>
> MY EVALUATION ☐☐☐☐

SPEAKING ■ Making, accepting and refusing invitations

6 Complete the dialogue with the words in the box.

> can't   pity   centre   busy   What   good
> want   about

Clare   Hey, Luke. Do you ¹_____ to go to the park after school?

Luke   No, sorry, Clare I ²_____. I've got a geography test tomorrow.

Clare   That's a ³_____.

Luke   Yeah.

Clare   What ⁴_____ Saturday then? Are you ⁵_____?

Luke   No, I'm not. Why? ⁶_____ are you doing?

Clare   I'm going to the shopping ⁷_____ if you want to come.

Luke   Sounds ⁸_____. Text me on Saturday morning. OK?

> **I can make, accept and refuse invitations.**
>
> MY EVALUATION ☐☐☐☐

WRITING ■ An email about school

7 Choose the correct answers.

1 Here's _____ information about my school.
   a any   b some   c a   d an

2 School starts _____ 8.30 every day.
   a with   b on   c at   d for

3 The classes are 50 minutes _____.
   a long   b big   c last   d large

4 _____ students study maths, English and science.
   a Every   b Any   c Much   d All

5 We can _____ other subjects like French.
   a choose   b stay   c listen   d write

6 There are some good clubs _____ school.
   a on   b after   c with   d about

7 You can buy snack food such _____ pizza.
   a like   b example   c for   d as

> **I can write an email about my school.**
>
> MY EVALUATION ☐☐☐☐

VOCABULARY ● Jobs

1 ★ Correct the words.

artist ___musician___

1 doctor _____

2 musician _____

3 king _____

4 actor _____

5 queen _____

6 scientist _____

7 writer _____

2 ★★ Complete the sentences with the words in the box.

> ~~businesswoman~~ explorer hairdresser
> waiter teacher chef mechanic
> farmer nurse builder firefighter

A ___businesswoman___ works in an office.

1 A _____ makes new houses and buildings.

2 A _____ takes food to people in a restaurant.

3 A _____ works with cars in a garage.

4 A _____ cuts and washes people's hair.

5 An _____ visits new countries.

6 A _____ helps children learn things.

7 A _____ works with animals and grows food for people.

8 A _____ stops fires in houses and buildings.

9 A _____ cooks food in a restaurant.

10 A _____ helps people in a hospital.

3 ★★ Do the *Famous People* quiz.

Famous People

Marie Curie was an important _____ from Poland.
a scientist **b** queen **c** artist

1 Henry VIII was an English _____ with six wives.
a doctor **b** king **c** explorer

2 Claude Monet and Paul Cézanne were _____ from France.
a musicians **b** artists **c** inventors

3 Charles Dickens and Jane Austen were British _____.
a writers **b** actors **c** doctors

4 Leonardo da Vinci was a famous Italian _____.
a mechanic **b** explorer **c** inventor

5 James Dean, Paul Newman and Humphrey Bogart were _____ from the USA.
a musicians **b** teachers **c** actors

6 Cleopatra was a famous _____ from ancient Egypt.
a scientist **b** artist **c** queen

4 ★★★ Make the words in the box into jobs and add them to the table. Use a dictionary to help you.

> empire violin ~~write~~ politics ~~music~~
> report magic sail photograph
> mathematics reception design ~~science~~
> dental ~~act~~ direct

-er	-or	-ist	-ian
writer	actor	scientist	musician

was, were

1 ⭐ **Complete the table with the words in the box.**

> wasn't   were   Was   weren't   was
> weren't   ~~was~~   Were   wasn't   were

Affirmative
I / He / She / It ¹ __was__ at home last night.
You / We / You / They ² _____ at the match.

Negative
I / He / She / It ³ _____ at school yesterday.
You / We / You / They ⁴ _____ at the party.

Questions
⁵ _____ I / he / she / it in Berlin last week?
⁶ _____ you / we / you / they in class?

Short answers	
Affirmative	**Negative**
Yes, I / he / she ⁷ _____.	No, I / he / she ⁹ _____.
Yes, you / we / they ⁸ _____.	No, you / we / they ¹⁰ _____.

2 ⭐⭐ **Correct the sentences.**

Leonardo da Vinci was French. (Italian)

__Leonardo da Vinci wasn't French. He was Italian.__

1 Elvis Presley was from Spain. (the USA)

_____

_____

2 Pablo Picasso was a musician. (artist)

_____

_____

3 The 2008 Olympics were in London. (Beijing)

_____

_____

4 Charles Darwin and Albert Einstein were interested in shopping. (science)

_____

_____

5 J.R.R. Tolkien was a famous actor. (writer)

_____

_____

6 John F. Kennedy and Abraham Lincoln were French presidents. (American)

_____

_____

3 ⭐⭐ **Order the words to make questions.**

birthday / his / was / February / in

__Was his birthday in February?__

1 bored / you / at / party / the / were

_____

2 football / was / match / when / the

_____

3 last / friends / where / your / night / were

_____

4 they / tired / were / morning / this

_____

5 was / what / your / name / grandmother's

_____

there was, there were

4 ⭐⭐ **Look at the picture. Write sentences with *there was*, *there wasn't*, *there were* and *there weren't*.**

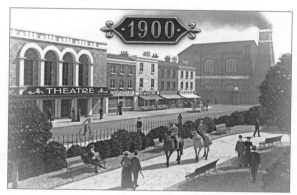

(shopping centre)

__In 1900 there wasn't a shopping centre.__

1 (shops) _____

2 (supermarket) _____

3 (cars) _____

4 (cinema) _____

5 (factory) _____

5 ⭐⭐⭐ **Write sentences about your town in 1900. Use *there was*, *there wasn't*, *there were*, *there weren't* and the words in the box.**

> cafés   park   car park   art gallery   ~~library~~
> hospital   flats   bus station   train station

__There was a library near the train station__ .

1 _____

2 _____

3 _____

4 _____

1 ⭐ **Find ten more verbs. Then write the past simple forms.**

I	N	V	A	D	E	B	C	R	O	S	S
N	C	J	O	V	K	S	H	P	I	Q	X
V	Y	N	A	M	E	X	A	L	H	V	T
E	B	L	U	I	W	H	N	B	Z	G	R
N	U	P	M	Z	Y	N	G	G	L	H	A
T	D	I	S	C	O	V	E	R	I	M	V
H	Z	J	Q	A	I	L	T	E	S	L	E
P	R	E	F	E	R	I	C	V	T	W	L
W	U	T	C	K	Z	V	Y	H	E	N	B
X	L	I	K	E	J	E	M	W	N	P	K

invade   _invaded_

1 _____ _____
2 _____ _____
3 _____ _____
4 _____ _____
5 _____ _____
6 _____ _____
7 _____ _____
8 _____ _____
9 _____ _____
10 _____ _____

2 ⭐⭐ **Complete the sentences using the past simple form of the verbs in the box.**

> change   discover   ~~invent~~   like   live
> name   travel   listen

Alexander Graham Bell ___invented___ the telephone.

1 When she was six, she _____ in Scotland.
2 Marie Curie _____ a new element, radium.
3 He _____ his name from Paul to Harry.
4 I _____ Mickey Mouse when I was a child.
5 We _____ our dog after a pop singer — he's called Mika.
6 On holiday last year, we _____ more than 1,000 kilometres.
7 They _____ to a radio programme about Marco Polo this morning.

3 ⭐⭐ **Choose the correct words.**

The Romans **travelled** /**invaded**/ **preferred** Britain in 55 BC.

1 John Logie Baird **listened** / **discovered** / **invented** the television.
2 When she was young, she **invaded** / **liked** / **lived** in Africa for five years.
3 Captain Cook **discovered** / **named** / **invented** Australia.
4 Last year we **travelled** / **invaded** / **discovered** by train to Rome.
5 My parents **crossed** / **changed** / **invented** their car in February.
6 That film about the Romans wasn't very good. We **preferred** / **named** / **lived** the other film.

4 ⭐⭐⭐ **Complete the postcard using the past simple form of some of the verbs in exercise 1.**

Hello Hattie!

I'm on holiday near Bologna in Italy with my family.

We ___crossed___ the English Channel by boat and we **1**_____ here by car – it's a long way! Yesterday, we were at the Marconi Museum – it's in a big house called the Villa Griffone, not far from Bologna.

Guglielmo Marconi is famous because he **2**_____ the radio. He **3**_____ in the Villa Griffone with his family when he was young.

We were at the museum all day, and we **4**_____ to a talk by a guide. I **5**_____ Villa Griffone a lot – it was really interesting. But my brother **6**_____ the Italian restaurant where we were last night. He doesn't like museums!

Love

Jennie

Past simple of regular verbs: affirmative and negative

1 ★ Complete the table with the words in the box.

> didn't visit   lived   didn't travel
> ~~travelled~~   visited   didn't live

Affirmative
I / You ¹ _travelled_ to London by plane yesterday.
We / You / They ² _____ in Rome last year.
He / She / It ³ _____ Paris two months ago.

Negative
I / You ⁴ _____ to London by train yesterday.
We / You / They ⁵ _____ in Berlin last year.
He / She / It ⁶ _____ Madrid two months ago.

2 ★★ Write sentences using the past simple affirmative and negative and the words in brackets.

Columbus / discover (Australia / America)

Columbus didn't discover Australia.
He discovered America.

1 Pelé / play (tennis / football)
_____

2 Queen Victoria / live (Poland / the UK)
_____
_____

3 Marconi / invent (the TV / the radio)
_____

4 In 1890 people / travel (by plane / by train)
_____
_____

5 The Romans / invade (America / France)
_____
_____

6 Neil Armstrong / explore (Antarctica / the moon)
_____
_____

Past time expressions

3 ★★ Order the words to make sentences. Use the past simple form of the verb.

three hours / watch / ago / I / TV

I watched TV three hours ago.

1 two months / she / her grandparents / ago / visit
_____
_____

2 arrive / Columbus / home / 1493 / in
_____

3 live / Mexico / last / in / you / year
_____

4 travel / James / a year / to Morocco / ago
_____

5 stay / hotel / I / yesterday / a / in
_____

6 that / watch / film / night / Jane / last
_____
_____

7 horses / people / century / use / the / in / 19th
_____
_____

4 ★★★ Write true sentences about you. Use the past simple affirmative and negative. Use the verbs and the time expressions.

> listen   play   stay   do   travel   visit
> watch   yesterday   two days ago   three
> weeks ago   last Friday   last night   last
> week   last month

I watched a DVD last night.

1 _____
2 _____
3 _____
4 _____
5 _____
6 _____
7 _____

CHRISTOFLE COLOMB, GENEVOIS
Chapitre 100.

1 ⭐ Read the text. The writer wrote this text to ...

a thank. **b** inform. **c** invite.

Famous scientists: The life of Marie Curie

A Marie Skłodowska was born in Warsaw, Poland, in 1867. She was one of five children. Marie's nickname as a child was 'Manya'. Her parents were both school teachers, but they were poor.

B Marie was a very clever child, but in Poland at that time girls didn't study at university. Her sister, Bronya, lived in Paris, so Marie moved there too. She started at the Sorbonne University and studied physics and mathematics.

C At the Sorbonne University, Marie worked with the scientist Pierre Curie. They married in 1895 and she changed her surname from Skłodowska to Curie. Marie and Pierre discovered the element radium in 1898.

D Pierre Curie died in 1906. Marie started teaching at the university. She was the first woman professor at the Sorbonne. She was also the first person to win two Nobel prizes.

E In the 1930s Marie was very ill because she worked with radioactive radium. She died in 1934.

2 ⭐⭐ Read the text again. Match topics 1–4 with paragraphs A–E.

The work of Marie and Pierre Curie. __C__

1 The early years. _____
2 The end of her life. _____
3 Teaching at the Sorbonne. _____
4 A new life in Paris. _____

3 ⭐⭐ Read the text again. Are the sentences *true* or *false*?

Marie's family was poor when she was a child. __true__

1 Marie's father was an inventor and her mother was a writer. _____
2 Marie's sister, Bronya, lived in Warsaw. _____
3 Marie studied mathematics and physics at the Sorbonne University. _____
4 In 1895, Marie discovered radium. _____
5 Marie's sister Bronya died in Warsaw in 1906. _____
6 Marie was ill in the 1930s. _____

4 ⭐⭐⭐ Answer the questions. Write complete sentences.

When and where was Marie Curie born?
__Marie Curie was born in 1867 in Warsaw, Poland.__

1 What job did her parents do?
_____

2 When did Marie change her surname?
_____
_____

3 What did she and her husband discover?
_____

4 What did Marie do after her husband died?
_____

5 Why was she ill?
_____

6 When did she die?
_____

Build your vocabulary

5 ⭐⭐ Complete the sentences with the words in the box.

> brand name   middle name   first name
> ~~nickname~~   surname

1 When she was a child, Marie's __nickname__ was Manya.
2 Marie's husband's _____ was Pierre and his _____ was Curie.
3 Marie and Pierre Curie discovered radium. But radium isn't a _____ like Armani.
4 Marie had three names – Marie Salomea Curie. Salomea was her _____.

Language point: Time expressions

1 ⭐ Complete the sentences with the words in the box.

> ago century ~~ago~~ in today the 1960s

The Romans invaded Britain about 2,000 years ___ago___.

1 The Romans arrived in Britain _____ 55 BC.

2 In the 16th _____ the population of London was 120,000.

3 The Great Fire of London was about 350 years _____.

4 People liked London in _____ because it was a very exciting city.

5 London is a big, modern city _____.

2 ⭐⭐ Complete the text with the words in the box.

> 1967   fifty years ago   ~~AD 75~~   today
> two hundred years   1970s

The Romans in Britain

Fishbourne Palace is an ancient monument in the south of England. Many people lived there in Roman times. The Romans started building the palace in ___AD 75___. People lived there for about ¹_____. People discovered Fishbourne again ²_____. In ³_____ they opened Fishbourne to the public and in the ⁴_____ a lot of people started to visit it. ⁵_____ 80,000 people go to the palace every year to see the mosaics.

◯ TASK

3 ⭐⭐ Read the notes about a Roman villa. Then complete the text.

Ancient monument: Chedworth Roman Villa
Location: near Gloucester, in the west of England
Built in: AD 120
Home of: a large, rich Roman family
Size: bigger than most other Roman villas in the UK
People lived there: for about three hundred years

TODAY
Discovered: 1864
Opened to the public: 1925
Things to see: beautiful Roman baths, mosaics
Visitors: popular with schools – 10,000 children visit every year

Chedworth Roman Villa is ___an ancient___ ___monument___ near Gloucester, ¹_____. It was the home of a large, rich Roman family. Chedworth Villa was very large – it ²_____. People ³_____. People discovered the villa ⁴_____ and in 1925 they ⁵_____. There are interesting things to see, such as ⁶_____. Today, the villa is very popular for school visits and ⁷_____.

4 ⭐⭐⭐ Read the notes and write a short text about Pompeii in Italy.

Place:	the town of Pompeii
Location:	Near Naples, in Italy
Home of:	many families in Roman times
Discovered:	1748
Opened to the public:	in the late 18th century
Size:	a small town
Things to see:	interesting Roman buildings, Roman baths and beautiful mosaics
Visitors:	over two million a year

VOCABULARY ● Jobs

1 Complete the words in the sentences.

1 My dad is a c _ _ _. He cooks in a French restaurant.

2 What's the name of the a _ _ _ _ in that film?

3 Henry VIII was a famous k _ _ _ of England.

4 My friend is a m _ _ _ _ _ _ _. She plays the piano and the guitar.

5 My grandfather is good at drawing. He's an a _ _ _ _ _.

6 I want to make new and exciting things when I'm older. I want to be an i _ _ _ _ _ _ _.

7 I work with cars. I'm a m _ _ _ _ _ _ _.

8 My sister works at the hospital near here. She's a n _ _ _ _.

> **I can talk about jobs.**
>
> MY EVALUATION ◯◯◯◯

READING ● The history of English names

2 Complete the dialogues with the words in the box.

> middle names   first name   surname
> nickname   brand name

1 What's your _____?
It's Anna.

2 Have you got any _____?
Yes, I've got two – Maria and Elizabeth.

3 Have you got a _____ for your brother?
Yes, I call him Bibi. It's not his real name.

4 Is your _____ Smith?
Yes, it's very common in the UK.

5 Is Prada a good name for a child?
No, it isn't – it's a _____.

> **I can understand an article about the history of names.**
>
> MY EVALUATION ◯◯◯◯

LANGUAGE FOCUS ● *was, were*

3 Complete the sentences with *was, were, wasn't* or *weren't*.

1 _____ that new DVD interesting?

2 My favourite singer last year _____ Rihanna.

3 _____ you at the party on Saturday?

4 Don't worry! The exam _____ difficult!

5 Who _____ your favourite teachers at primary school?

6 My parents don't like art. They _____ interested in the art gallery.

7 My best friends last year _____ Susie and Kate.

8 David is in hospital. He _____ at the football match today.

> **I can talk about the past with *was* and *were*.**
>
> MY EVALUATION ◯◯◯◯

VOCABULARY AND LISTENING ● Strange Town USA

4 Complete the sentences with one of the verbs in the past simple.

1 Columbus _____ the Atlantic Ocean in the 15th century. (invade / cross / change)

2 People _____ gold in South Africa hundreds of years ago. (discover / invent / invade)

3 The Romans _____ different countries in Europe. (invent / invade / travel)

4 László Bíró _____ the ballpoint pen. (discover / change / invent)

5 Norma Jean Baker _____ her name to Marilyn Monroe. (invent / change / cross)

6 My grandparents _____ (travel / invade / like) to India last year.

> **I can understand an interview about how people named some American towns.**
>
> MY EVALUATION ◯◯◯◯

LANGUAGE FOCUS ■ Past simple of regular verbs

5 Write sentences in the past simple affirmative or negative.

1 In 1600 / people / not travel / by train

_____

2 Cleopatra / live / in Egypt / two thousand years ago

_____

_____

3 Marconi / not invent / the internet

_____

4 The astronaut Yuri Gagarin / visit / space / in 1961

_____

_____

5 Ferdinand Magellan / not discover / Australia

_____

_____

6 Travellers / stop using / horses / a hundred years ago

_____

_____

> **I can talk about my past experiences.**
>
> MY EVALUATION ☐☐☐☐

SPEAKING ■ Last weekend

6 Match questions 1–6 with answers a–f.

1 How was your weekend? _____
2 Were you on your own? _____
3 What was Edinburgh like? _____
4 What was the hotel like? _____
5 What about the tourist sites? _____
6 Was your weekend good? _____

a No, I was with my family.
b It was cool. The shops and parks were nice.
c Really brilliant. I was in Edinburgh.
d Yes, it was. Thank you.
e It was small and modern with great food.
f They were fantastic. We visited lots of art galleries.

> **I can talk about my weekend.**
>
> MY EVALUATION ☐☐☐☐

WRITING ■ An article about a town

7 Complete the text with the words in the box.

> include   century   population   people
> ago   called   River   city   lived

Birmingham is a ¹_____ in the centre of England. It is on the ²_____ Rea.

People first ³_____ in Birmingham more than a thousand years ⁴_____. In those days it was ⁵_____ Brummagem and it wasn't very big. In the 17th ⁶_____ only 15,000 people lived there. Today the ⁷_____ is over a million.

The ⁸_____ of Birmingham are called 'Brummies'. Famous people from Birmingham ⁹_____ the writer J.R.R. Tolkien and the singer Ozzy Osbourne.

> **I can write about a place and its history.**
>
> MY EVALUATION ☐☐☐☐

7 ☐☐☐☐☐☐☐☐ Games

VOCABULARY ■ Sport

1 ⟨★⟩ **Match sentence halves 1–8 with a–h.**

1 Paula Radcliffe ran   _b_
2 Lionel Messi scored   ___
3 Roger Federer played   ___
4 Lewis Hamilton won   ___
5 Manchester United lost   ___
6 Serena Williams beat   ___
7 Michael Phelps broke   ___
8 My best friend took   ___

a her sister at tennis.
b a race in New York.
c a game 1–0.
d two goals last night.
e a motor race yesterday.
f some world records.
g part in a competition.
h a game against Rafael Nadal.

2 ⟨★★⟩ **Look at the photos. Complete the sentences using the past simple form of the words in the box.**

> beat   break   win   ~~take part~~   score   lose

They __took part__ in a marathon last week.

1 He _____ a world record last year.

2 She _____ the game last Sunday.

3 He _____ a goal earlier.

4 She _____ her friend at tennis.

5 He _____ the race yesterday.

3 ⟨★★⟩ **Choose the correct answers.**

When I'm older I want to _____ a world record.
a score   b run   (c break)   d play

1 I often _____ my brother at table tennis.
   a win   b score   c beat   d break
2 Our school basketball team never _____ a match.
   a loses   b runs   c takes   d scores
3 I sometimes _____ part in swimming competitions.
   a play   b take   c break   d win
4 My favourite footballer always _____ a lot of goals.
   a beats   b takes   c plays   d scores
5 We often _____ 200m races at school.
   a play   b run   c beat   d take
6 I sometimes _____ tennis after school.
   a play   b score   c break   d run

4 ⟨★★★⟩ **Complete the text with sport verbs in the past simple.**

Usain Bolt

Usain Bolt comes from a small town in Jamaica. He was first interested in sport when he was a child. He often ___played___ games of football with his brother and his friends. He usually ¹_____ a lot of goals because he was very fast and strong.

Bolt loved running and he ²_____ part in competitions when he was at school. He always ³_____ the races and ⁴_____ all the other boys in his class.

When he was older Bolt ⁵_____ in a lot of races for his country and he first ⁶_____ the 100m world record in New York in 2008.

1 ★ Complete the table with the past simple form of the verbs.

Regular	
Infinitive	**Past simple**
design	1 _designed_
like	2 _____
listen	3 _____
play	4 _____

Irregular	
Infinitive	**Past simple**
buy	5 _____
have	6 _____
go	7 _____
know	8 _____
make	9 _____
write	10 _____

2 ★★ Write sentences. Make the affirmative sentences negative and the negative sentences affirmative.

They played basketball after school.

They didn't play basketball after school.

1 You didn't win the race yesterday.

_____

2 She knew the answer to the question.

_____

_____

3 We didn't go to the football match.

_____

4 I liked that video game.

_____

5 They didn't buy tickets for the concert.

_____

_____

6 Amy ate a lot before the big race.

_____

_____

7 He didn't design the new computer.

_____

_____

8 I met Simon at the tennis competition.

_____

_____

3 ★★ Complete the text. Use the past simple affirmative or negative form of the words in the boxes.

> see   travel   ~~buy~~

One summer my dad __bought__ two tickets to watch tennis at Wimbledon. Dad and I
¹_____ to London by train and we
²_____ Roger Federer and Rafael Nadal in the men's final.

> play   lose   not win

The match was very long and they ³_____ for four hours and forty-eight minutes! My dad thinks Federer is a great player, but Federer
⁴_____ – he ⁵_____ the game at 9.15 p.m. Nadal was the champion.

> have   not eat   go

After the match we went to a restaurant for dinner.
I ⁶_____ a burger, but my dad ⁷_____ anything. We didn't go home because it was 11.15 p.m. and the last train was at 10.30 p.m. We stayed in a hotel and
⁸_____ home in the morning.

4 ★★★ Think about last year. Write about six things that happened to you. Use affirmative and negative forms of the verbs in the box.

> go on holiday   win a competition
> meet new friends   have a party
> play volleyball   take part in a race
> travel by plane   buy a new CD

I won a competition in March.

1 _____

2 _____

3 _____

4 _____

5 _____

6 _____

VOCABULARY ■ Describing people

1 ★ Choose the correct words.

My sister's got blonde hair and ⟨blue⟩/ red eyes.

1 Susanna is **quite** / **average** height. She's got dark hair and brown eyes.

2 Our teacher has got **glasses** / **beard** and a moustache.

3 Katie is tall and **slim** / **curly** and she's got brown eyes.

4 Mark is average height and average build. He's got **fair** / **green** eyes and curly hair.

5 Their children have got **average** / **red** hair and green eyes.

6 My dad has got a beard but he hasn't got a **moustache** / **glasses**.

7 Sam is one metre eighty-five. He's **short** / **tall** and he's slim.

8 Joseph is quite **short** / **blonde** and he's got dark hair.

9 Toni and Harry have got **brown** / **average** eyes.

10 My mum has got **dark** / **fat** hair.

2 ★★ Complete the words in the description.

My name's Ella and I'm sixteen years old. I've got green eyes and I've got ¹g_____. I'm quite ²t_____ and I'm average ³b_____. My sister Hannah is ten. She's ⁴q_____ short and she's ⁵s_____. Our dad's name is Tony. He's ⁶a_____ height and he's got a ⁷b_____. Our mum's name is Sandra. She's got ⁸f_____ hair and blue eyes.

3 ★★ Look at the photo. Describe Nicole Kidman.

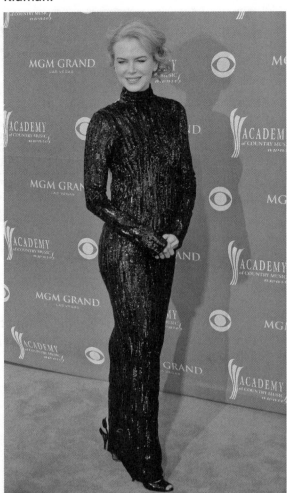

eye colour   _She's got blue eyes._____

1 height   _____

2 build   _____

3 hair (colour)   _____

4 hair   _____

4 ★★★ Write five sentences to describe yourself.

_I'm tall and I'm average build._____

1 _____
_____

2 _____
_____

3 _____
_____

4 _____
_____

5 _____
_____

1 ★ Complete the table with the words in the box.

> Did   did   buy   ~~Did~~   didn't   did   go   didn't

Question
¹**Did** I / you / we / you / they win?

Short answers	
Affirmative	**Negative**
Yes, I / you / we / you / they ²_____.	No, I / you / we / you / they ³_____.

Question
⁴_____ he / she / it lose?

Short answers	
Affirmative	**Negative**
Yes, he / she / it ⁵_____.	No, he / she / it ⁶_____.

Questions
Where did I / you / we / you / they ⁷_____?
What did he / she / it ⁸_____ at the shops?

2 ★★ Complete the past simple questions and short answers. Use *did / didn't* and the words in the box.

> win   eat   break   do   play   write   ~~watch~~

_____**Did**_____ you ___**watch**___ a good film on TV last night?

No, I ___**didn't**___.

1 _____ she _____ the 200m race on Saturday?
Yes, she _____.

2 _____ he _____ in the football team last week?
No, he _____.

3 _____ you _____ a lot of homework last night?
No, I _____.

4 _____ they _____ a lot of cake?
Yes, they _____.

5 _____ we _____ a letter and say 'thank you'?
Yes, we _____.

6 _____ she _____ the world record yesterday?
No, she _____.

3 ★★ Look at the words and pictures and write past simple questions.

what / they / eat / ?
What did they eat?

1 what time / he / get up /?
_____

2 who / she / visit / ?
_____

3 what / she / play / ?
_____

4 where / they / go / on holiday / ?
_____

5 when / he / start school / ?
_____

4 ★★★ Read the answers about Wayne Rooney's day. Write the questions.

> Yes, I played football yesterday morning.
>
> **1** I had lunch at my mum's house.
>
> **2** I ate pasta for dinner.
>
> **3** I watched a film in the evening.
>
> **4** Yes, I liked the film. It was funny.
>
> **5** Yes, Coleen watched the film with me.
>
> **6** I went to bed at 11.00 p.m.

<u>Did you play football yesterday morning?</u>

1 _____
2 _____
3 _____
4 _____
5 _____
6 _____

READING ■ A famous game

1 ★ Read the text. Tick ✔ the correct box.

The text is about …

a ☐ a design
b ☐ an inventor
c ☐ a game

The Rubik's Cube

A My name's Ben. I'm twelve years old and I want to design games. Why? Because I love the Rubik's Cube! It's my favourite game of all time and I can do it in three minutes.

B The cube has got six colours: white, yellow, orange, red, blue and green. To play it you move the cube and make each side one colour.

C Ernö Rubik is the creator of the Rubik's Cube. He created it in 1974 and it quickly became a popular game. Millions of people bought it all over the world.

D My dad started playing with the Rubik's Cube in the 1980s. All his friends were into it too. Today there are three players in our house: me, my dad and my little sister, Molly. She can't do it, but that's OK because I help her.

E Ernö Rubik invented something he really liked and made money from it. I want to design new games too — maybe a more popular game! I've got a lot of good ideas!

2 ★★ Read the text again. Match topics 1–4 with paragraphs A–E.

Ben introduces himself.   <u>A</u>

1 Ben's ideas for new games.   ____
2 He talks about the inventor of the game and when he invented it.   ____
3 He describes the game.   ____
4 Ben says who plays the game in his family.   ____

3 ★★ Read the text again. Complete the sentences with the words in the box.

> created   ideas   design   ~~favourite~~   helps
> does   colours   popular

The Rubik's Cube is Ben's ___favourite___ game.

1 There are six _____ in the cube.
2 Ben _____ the cube in three minutes.
3 Ernö Rubik _____ the cube.
4 The game was very_____ in the 1970s.
5 Ben _____ his sister with the cube.
6 Ben wants to _____ new games.
7 Ben has got some _____ for games.

4 ★★★ Answer the questions. Write complete sentences.

Who invented the Rubik's Cube?
<u>Ernö Rubik invented the Rubik's Cube.</u>

1 How many people bought the Rubik's Cube?
_____

2 What colours are in the cube?
_____

3 When did Rubik first make the cube?
_____

4 When did Ben's dad start playing with the Rubik's Cube?
_____
_____

5 Can Molly do the Rubik's Cube?
_____

6 What does Ben want to do in the future?
_____

Build your vocabulary

5 ★★ Choose the correct words.

1 My sister (designs) / designers computer games.
2 Do you want to **play** / **player** my new video game?
3 Video games are good **entertain** / **entertainment**.
4 Did you **create** / **creator** that new game?
5 Have you got a good **remember** / **memory** for people's names?
6 You can **choose** / **choice** this game or that game.
7 You need a good **imagine** / **imagination** when you write a children's book.

Language point: *also*

1 ★ **Order the words to make sentences.**

You are good at sport.

also / good / you / are / art / at

<u>You are also good at art.</u>

1 She's into music.
likes / she / reading / also

_____

2 I walk to school.
to / walk / also / I / shops / the

_____

3 He was a writer.
an / also / inventor / was / he

_____

4 You speak Italian.
speak / you / English / also

_____

5 She has got brown eyes.
hair / brown / she / got / also / has

_____

2 ★★ **Rewrite the second sentence with *also*.**

She is good at French. She is good at Spanish.

<u>She is also good at Spanish.</u>

1 He likes science. He is interested in history.

_____

2 They went to the beach. They visited a friend.

_____

_____

3 He has got blue eyes. He is very tall.

_____

4 I ate an apple. I had a banana.

_____

5 She is clever. She is very nice.

_____

6 We run every day. We play volleyball.

_____

_____

○ TASK

3 ★★ **Complete the text. Use the information in the box.**

I won my first Paralympic medal in 1988 in Seoul, Korea.
I've got one daughter.
My middle name is Davina.
I started doing wheelchair athletics when I was thirteen.
My daughter was born in 2002.
I was born in Wales.

My life

I was born on 26 July 1969 in Cardiff, <u>Wales</u>.
My full name is Carys ¹_____ Grey-Thompson, but my nickname is Tanni. My sister gave me the nickname.

My sport

I'm an athlete and I've got a lot of medals. I started to use a wheelchair when I was seven. When I was ²_____ I started doing wheelchair athletics.
I won my first ³_____ medal in 1988, in ⁴_____.
In 2004 I won two gold medals at the Athens Paralympic Games.

My family

I live in the north-east of England with my family.
My husband's name is Ian and we've got one ⁵_____.
She was born in ⁶_____ and her name is Carys. She loves the colour pink!

4 ★★★ **Write a profile of a famous person or someone you know.**
Put the information into three paragraphs:

His / Her life   His / Her sport or interest   His / Her family

MY EVALUATION   Check your progress. Do the exercises and then complete your own evaluation.

◼◻◻◻ *I need to try this again.*   ◼◼◼◻ *I am happy with this.*

◼◼◻◻ *I could do this better.*   ◼◼◼◼ *I can do this very well.*

VOCABULARY ● Sport

1 Complete the sentences with one of the verbs in the past simple.

1 She _____ the 1,500m record again last week. (score / play / break)

2 You _____ an amazing goal yesterday. (win / score / beat)

3 James often _____ races at school when he was younger. (beat / take / run)

4 They _____ part in a big volleyball competition last year. (take / break / play)

5 We _____ the football match 5–0. (score / beat / lose)

6 I _____ my dad at that computer game. (win / beat / break)

7 He _____ a game of basketball with his new team. (play / take / run)

8 Lily _____ the important race on Sunday. (beat / score / win)

> **I can talk about sports and sports events.**
> MY EVALUATION ◻◻◻◻

READING ● Video games

2 Complete the sentences. Use the verbs in brackets to make new words.

1 Who is the _____ (design) of the game?

2 That writer has got a good _____ (imagine).

3 I like those video games. They're great _____ (entertain).

4 We can play The SIMS or Super Mario World – it's your _____ (choose).

5 The _____ (create) of this action game made a lot of money.

6 Have you got a good _____ (remember)?

7 How many _____ (play) can use that game?

> **I can understand an article about video games.**
> MY EVALUATION ◻◻◻◻

LANGUAGE FOCUS ● Past simple: regular and irregular verbs

3 Make the affirmative sentences negative and the negative sentences affirmative.

1 We didn't have breakfast this morning.
_____

2 I went to the museum.
_____

3 He didn't listen to the teacher.
_____

4 She made a cake.
_____

5 You didn't write a letter.
_____

6 They became very famous.
_____

7 She didn't know my name.
_____

8 I met my friends.
_____

> **I can talk about actions in the past.**
> MY EVALUATION ◻◻◻◻

VOCABULARY AND LISTENING ●
Describing people

4 Complete the words in the sentences.

1 Anna isn't very tall. She's a _ _ _ _ _ _ height.

2 Is his hair curly?
No, it's s _ _ _ _ _ _ _.

3 I can't read this book. I need to wear my g _ _ _ _ _ _.

4 What colour is her hair?
It's r _ _.

5 They aren't fat. They're quite s _ _ _.

6 I've got f _ _ _ hair and b _ _ _ eyes.

7 My dad has got a black b _ _ _ _ and a big m _ _ _ _ _ _ _.

> **I can describe people's appearance.**
> MY EVALUATION ◻◻◻◻

LANGUAGE FOCUS ■ Past simple: questions

5 Write past simple questions.

1 what / you / do / yesterday

_____

2 where / you / go

_____

3 your sister / like / the film

_____

4 your parents / buy / the tickets

_____

5 you / go / by train

_____

6 what time / they / eat

_____

7 your brother / do / his homework

_____

8 when / you / go / to bed

_____

9 you / play / volleyball / yesterday

_____

10 who / you / see / at school

_____

> **I can ask and answer questions about last weekend.**
>
> MY EVALUATION ☐☐☐☐

SPEAKING ■ Talking about past events

6 Order the sentences to make a dialogue.

a ☐ Luke I went to my friend's house to play computer games. It was brilliant!

b ☐ Ollie OK. Why not?

c ☐ Ollie Not really. I didn't do anything. What did you do?

d ☐ Luke Hi, Ollie. Did you have a good weekend?

e ☐ Luke Yes, we did! Why don't you come with me next time?

f ☐ Ollie That's cool. Did you play all day?

> **I can talk about things I did last weekend.**
>
> MY EVALUATION ☐☐☐☐

WRITING ■ A profile

7 Read the sentences about motor racing driver Lewis Hamilton. Choose the correct answers.

1 His _____ name is Lewis Carl Davidson Hamilton.
   a brand **b** long **c** full **d** first

2 He _____ professional in 2001.
   a won **b** turned **c** broke **d** started

3 He _____ the Canadian Grand Prix in 2007.
   a beat **b** scored **c** played **d** won

4 He's _____ dark hair and brown eyes.
   a got **b** have **c** wear **d** look

5 He was born _____ 7th January 1985.
   a in **b** on **c** at **d** for

6 He _____ drove a car when he was six years old.
   a now **b** last **c** first **d** early

7 He _____ won the world championship in 2008.
   a also **b** too **c** more **d** and

> **I can write a profile of a famous sportsperson.**
>
> MY EVALUATION ☐☐☐☐

8 ▪︎▪︎▪︎▫︎▫︎▫︎ Expedition

VOCABULARY ▪ Travel equipment

1 ★ **Complete the crossword.**

ACROSS

1 2 3

5 6 8

DOWN

1 4 7

Crossword: 1 S U N S C R E E N

2 ★★ **Read the clues and write the objects.**

> insect repellent   rope   sunglasses
> gloves   helmet   satellite phone
> ~~tent~~   waterproof clothes

A small house; people sleep inside it.
___tent___

1 Insects don't like this. _____
2 This is very long; it helps you go up a mountain. _____
3 Use this to talk to your family. _____
4 These protect your eyes when there is a lot of sun. _____
5 When it rains, these help you to stay dry. _____
6 These protect your hands. _____
7 This hat protects your head. _____

3 ★★ **Complete the sentences with words in exercise 1.**

My foot is bad. Where's the _first aid kit_?

1 Look at your _____ to find north.
2 It's very sunny. Put on some _____.
3 Let's cook some food. Where's the _____?
4 I'm tired. Where's my _____?
5 We're lost. Have you got a _____?
6 All my clothes are in my _____.

4 ★★★ **Complete the postcard.**

Hi Ellie,

I'm on an expedition in the rainforests of Australia. There are four of us on the trip and we sleep in a big ___tent___. I've got a comfortable ¹_____ and I always sleep well. It's really dark at night, but I've got a good ²_____ with me. I carry my clothes and things in a large ³_____. It's very hot and sunny in the day, so I must put ⁴_____ on my face. Also, I always use a lot of ⁵_____ because there are millions of insects here!

I talk to my mum on the ⁶_____ every day!

See you soon!
Emily x

Imperatives

1 ★★ Complete the sentences using the affirmative or negative imperative form of the words in the box.

> be ~~buy~~ drink eat go wear
> look use write

___Don't buy___ that rucksack. It's very small and the colour is horrible.

1 Where's the cinema?
_____ to the station. It's near there.

2 Please _____ your name and telephone number here.

3 _____ water from the river! It isn't clean.

4 _____! There's a big bear in that tree.

5 _____ my laptop. I'm going to do my homework on it.

6 Please _____ quiet, children! You're talking a lot today.

7 _____ that sandwich. It's three weeks old!

8 _____ sunscreen every day on holiday!

be going to: affirmative and negative

2 ★ Complete the table with the words in the box.

> Am Are aren't Is isn't ~~'m~~
> 'm not 're 's

Affirmative
I ¹ _'m_ going to travel.
He / She / It ² _____ going to eat.
You / We / You / They ³ _____ going to stay.

Negative
I ⁴ _____ going to study.
He / She / It ⁵ _____ going to play.
You / We / You / They ⁶ _____ going to read.

Questions
⁷ _____ I going to see you?
⁸ _____ he / she / it going to start?
⁹ _____ you / we / you / they going to cook?

3 ★★ Paul, John, Lara and Mary are going to Sri Lanka this summer. Write affirmative and negative sentences using *be going to*.

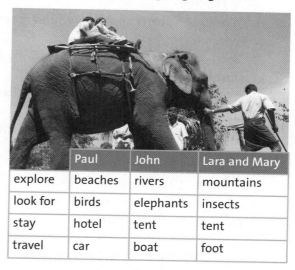

	Paul	John	Lara and Mary
explore	beaches	rivers	mountains
look for	birds	elephants	insects
stay	hotel	tent	tent
travel	car	boat	foot

John ___is going to explore___ the rivers of Sri Lanka.

Paul ___isn't going to look for___ elephants.

1 Lara and Mary _____ the mountains.

2 Paul _____ the beautiful beaches.

3 John _____ new species of birds.

4 Lara and Mary _____ in a hotel.

5 Paul _____ in a tent.

6 John _____ in a tent.

7 Lara and Mary _____ by car.

8 John _____ by boat.

4 ★★★ What are you going to do at the weekend? Write true affirmative and negative sentences about you and your family. Use the words in the box or your own ideas.

> tennis DVD homework grandparents
> computer games TV friends dinner

___I'm going to watch a DVD on Saturday.___

___My dad isn't going to play tennis.___

1 _____
2 _____
3 _____
4 _____
5 _____

(*be going to* questions practice ⇨ page 67)

1 ⭐ **Choose the correct words.**

We cancelled our skiing holiday. There isn't any **snowy** / snow .

1 Take some sunscreen. It's very **sunny** / **sun** today.
2 Don't go out today. There's a big **stormy** / **storm**.
3 It isn't raining, but it's quite **cloudy** / **cloud**.
4 I prefer **hot** / **heat** weather.
5 The roads are very dangerous today – there's **icy** / **ice** and **foggy** / **fog**.
6 What's the weather like?
   Horrible. It's cold and **rainy** / **rain**.
7 It isn't cold today. The **windy** / **wind** is coming from the south.

2 ⭐⭐ **Label the weather symbols with the adjectives in exercise 1.**

_____rainy_____

1 _____

2 _____

3 _____

4 _____

5 _____

6 _____

7 _____

8 _____

9 _____

3 ⭐⭐ **Look at the weather forecast map and complete the sentences. Use the adjectives in exercise 1.**

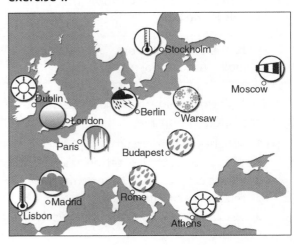

It's _____sunny_____ in Athens and Dublin today.

1 It's _____ in Budapest and Rome.
2 It's _____ in Warsaw right now.
3 At the moment it's _____ in Moscow.
4 It's _____ in Lisbon.
5 It's _____ in London right now.
6 It's _____ in Berlin today.
7 At the moment it's _____ in Madrid.
8 It's _____ in Stockholm today.
9 It's _____ in Paris at the moment.

4 ⭐⭐⭐ **Imagine you are in these places. Write sentences about the weather.**

The Alps in winter.
It's cold. There's lots of snow and ice.

1 The Sahara desert at night.
_____

2 The Amazon rainforest.
_____

3 The Antarctic in summer.
_____

4 The Caribbean in September.
_____

5 Where you live in April.
_____

6 Where you live in January.
_____

be going to: questions

1 ⭐⭐ Write questions about a holiday in New York using *be going to*. Then match questions 1–6 with answers a–f.

where / you / stay / in New York / ?

<u>Where are you going to stay in New York?</u>   e

1 what / your brother / do / there / ?

_____

_____ __

2 what / you / buy / ?

_____

_____ __

3 what / places / you / visit / ?

_____

_____ __

4 where / you / eat / ?

_____

_____ __

5 how / you / travel / in New York / ?

_____

_____ __

6 you / take / a lot of photos / ?

_____

_____ __

a By cab and subway.
b A New York Yankees baseball cap.
c The Statue of Liberty and Central Park.
d In some New York 'diner' restaurants.
e At my cousin's apartment in Manhattan.
f Yes, I am. I've got a new camera.
g See a baseball game.

will and *won't*

2 ⭐ Complete the table with the words in the box.

> won't ⁤𝐼𝐼 Will won't will play

Affirmative
I / You / He / She / It / We / You / They **1** _'ll_ win.
Negative
I / You / He / She / It /We / You / They **2** _____ lose.
Questions
3 _____ I / you / he / she / it / we / you / they **4** _____ tennis?

Short answers	
Affirmative	**Negative**
Yes, I / you / he / she / it / we / you / they **5** _____.	No, I / you / he / she / it / we / you / they **6** _____.

3 ⭐⭐ You are going on an expedition to the Amazon. Write questions or affirmative or negative sentences with *will* or *won't*.

it / be / very hot / in the Amazon
<u>It'll be very hot in the Amazon.</u>

1 we / see / a lot of / interesting animals
_____

2 I / not sleep / in a comfortable bed
_____

3 you / take / a lot of photos / ?
_____

4 Jess / not talk / on the satellite phone
_____

5 Mark / burn / in the sun
_____

4 ⭐⭐⭐ Write predictions about your country in the future. Think about the weather, animals, people, food, jobs, houses and schools. Use the words in the box to help you.

> become   change   be   live   eat   move
> work   buy   study   travel

<u>The weather will become hotter and more stormy.</u>

1 _____
2 _____
3 _____
4 _____

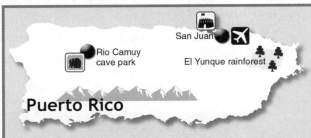

Puerto Rico

I'm going on holiday with my parents and my sister Sophie next week. We're going to Puerto Rico for two weeks — I'm really excited!

We're going to arrive at the International Airport on Saturday at 8.15 p.m. The airport is only fifteen minutes from San Juan. The tour guide is going to meet us and take us to our hotel — the Hotel

Isabela in Old San Juan. On the first day of the holiday we're going to visit the beaches in San Juan and relax.

The next day we're going to do a rainforest tour. The minibus is going to come to our hotel at 8.00 a.m. and take us to the El Yunque rainforest visitor centre. El Yunque is the home of beautiful parrots, enormous trees and amazing flowers. I'm going to take my waterproof clothes because I think it'll be rainy there.

For me, the most exciting day is Tuesday. It's the visit to the famous Rio Camuy caves, in the north-west of Puerto Rico. We'll wear strong shoes, because we're going to visit the caves for three hours with a guide!

1 ★ **Read the text. Tick ✓ the correct box.**

The text is about …

a ☐ a family camping expedition.

b ☐ two different family holidays.

c ☐ a family holiday.

2 ★★ **Choose the correct answers.**

The family are going to arrive on _____.

a Saturday b Sunday c Monday

1 The family are going to arrive at _____.
   a 8.00 a.m. b 8.15 p.m. c 8.45 a.m.

2 It is _____ from the airport to San Juan.
   a two hours b an hour
   c a quarter of an hour

3 San Juan is the name of a _____.
   a town b hotel c beach

4 They are going to travel to the rainforest by _____.

   a car b plane c minibus

5 In the rainforest they are going to go to a _____.

   a shop b visitor centre c cave

6 On Tuesday they are going to visit _____.
   a some caves b a hotel c a beach

3 ★★ **Read the text again. Are the sentences *true* or *false*?**

The airport is in San Juan.   *false*

1 A guide is going to meet them at the hotel.   _____

2 There aren't any beaches in San Juan. _____

3 On Tuesday the family are going to visit the rainforest.   _____

4 There are parrots in the rainforest.   _____

5 It's important to wear sandals in the caves.   _____

6 They are going to be in the caves for three hours.   _____

4 ★★★ **Complete the summary of the text.**

The text is about plans for a ___holiday___ in Puerto Rico. The family are going to arrive at the ¹_____ and then go to the ²_____ in San Juan.

On the first day of their holiday, they're going to go to the ³_____ but they want to see other places too.

They're going to visit the ⁴_____ in the north of Puerto Rico. They also want to explore the beautiful green ⁵_____ and go to the visitor ⁶_____ there.

Build your vocabulary

5 ★★ **Complete the sentences with the words in the box.**

miserable scared ~~worried~~ angry
lucky excited

We've got an exam tomorrow and I'm __worried__.

1 Are you _____ of snakes?

2 My brother took my bike. I'm _____.

3 My dad won the lottery. He's _____!

4 I'm going to see my cousin. I'm _____.

5 Her dog died and she's _____.

Language point: *so*

1 ★ Choose the correct words.

It's rainy today, (so) / but I'm going to wear my waterproof clothes.

1 My mother doesn't like spiders **so / or** flies.

2 I'm very cold, **or / so** I'm going to get in my sleeping bag.

3 I want an ice cream, **so / but** I haven't got any money.

4 I like Carolina **because / so** she's really friendly.

5 I'm tired, **but / so** I'm going to go to bed.

6 I'm hungry, **so / because** I'm going to make a sandwich.

7 We're going to walk in the mountains **so / or** play football.

8 There's a good film on TV tonight, **so / because** we're going to watch it.

2 ★★ Rewrite the sentences with *so*.

I'm very hot. I'm going to swim in the river.

I'm very hot so I'm going to swim in the river.

1 I'm good at maths. I'm going to help Amy with her homework.

_____

2 Maria hasn't got a bike. She always walks to school.

_____

3 Charlie likes Italian food. He's going to have pasta.

_____

4 It's snowy and cold. I'm going to wear my big coat.

_____

5 I haven't got a mobile phone. I can't speak to my family.

_____

6 It's very sunny. We're going to put on some sunscreen.

_____

○ TASK

3 ★★ Georgia is going on a day trip with her school. Read the notes and complete her email.

School trip: York
Place: the city of York
When: Friday 10th July
Time: Bus leaves 6.30 a.m., returns 8.30 p.m.
Weather: hot and sunny
Things to take: sunscreen, new sunglasses
Things to see: cathedral, National Railway Museum

4 ★★★ Imagine you are going to go on a school trip. Make notes in the table. Then write an email about your trip.

School trip	
Place	
When	
Time	
Weather	
Things to take	
Things to see	

Delete Reply Reply All Forward New Mailboxes Get Mail

Hi, Hannah!

How are you? I'm very excited because I'm going to **visit the city of York** on Friday with my school.

We're going to travel ¹_____. We ²_____ at 6.30 a.m. and return at about ³_____.

I looked at the weather forecast on TV – it's going to be really ⁴_____, so ⁵_____. York has got a lot of interesting places to visit.

There's ⁶_____. You can see a lot of beautiful old trains there.

Bye for now,

Georgia

MY EVALUATION   Check your progress. Do the exercises and then complete your own evaluation.

■◻◻◻ I need to try this again.   ■■■◻ I am happy with this.

■■◻◻ I could do this better.   ■■■■ I can do this very well.

VOCABULARY ■ Travel equipment

1 Complete the words in the sentences.

1 It's very dark now! Where's the t _ _ _ _?

2 We're lost again. I'm going to look at the m _ _.

3 She's got a long r _ _ _ and she's going to climb a mountain.

4 I want to cook. Where's the s _ _ _ _?

5 Karl's hands are cold. He's going to put on some g _ _ _ _ _.

6 Do you like sleeping in a t _ _ _?

7 It's very sunny today. I want to put some s _ _ _ _ _ _ _ _ on my face.

8 This mountain is dangerous. I'm going to wear a h _ _ _ _ _ to protect my head.

> **I can talk about what to do on an expedition.**
>
> MY EVALUATION   ◻◻◻◻

READING ■ An adventure story

2 Choose the correct answers.

1 We won an expensive wildlife holiday last week. We were very _____!
a angry   b lucky   c scared   d miserable

2 Great! It's our holiday today! We're _____.
a worried   b angry   c miserable   d excited

3 She's _____ because she's really tired and hungry.
a lucky   b miserable   c scared   d excited

4 My sister has got my sunglasses again! I'm really _____ with her.
a lucky   b angry   c excited   d scared

5 I don't like spiders. I'm _____ of them.
a scared   b lucky   c angry   d miserable

6 We've got a dangerous walk tomorrow and we're _____.
a lucky   b miserable   c worried   d angry

> **I can understand an adventure story.**
>
> MY EVALUATION   ◻◻◻◻

LANGUAGE FOCUS ■ *be going to*

3 Complete the sentences using affirmative, negative or question forms of *be going to*.

1 They _____ (travel) to the islands by boat.

2 They _____ (not take) a tent.

3 He _____ (explore) the mountains.

4 What _____ (you / look for)?

5 How _____ (they / make) dinner?

6 I _____ (not swim) in the river.

7 We _____ (bring) a camera.

8 She _____ (look at) the map.

> **I can talk about plans and intentions.**
>
> MY EVALUATION   ◻◻◻◻

VOCABULARY AND LISTENING ■ Weather conditions

4 Complete the sentences with one of the words in brackets.

1 Do you like this _____ weather? (heat / hot)

2 It's cold today. There's _____ on the car. (icy / ice)

3 I can't see the sun because of that _____. (cloud / cloudy)

4 The weather on holiday was very _____. (stormy / storm).

5 Don't drive fast in the car. It's _____. (fog / foggy)

6 We can't ski. There isn't any _____. (snowy / snow)

7 There's a cold _____. Wear a coat. (wind / windy)

8 Have you got waterproof clothes? It's _____. (rain / rainy)

> **I can talk about the weather.**
>
> MY EVALUATION   ◻◻◻◻

LANGUAGE FOCUS ● *will* and *won't*

5 Complete the sentences using *will* or *won't* and the verbs in the box.

> not win   design   not go   become
> like   live

1 In the future, tigers _____ extinct.
2 She _____ to university. She never studies.
3 You _____ this DVD. It's really good.
4 _____ inventors _____ very fast planes?
5 He _____ any money. He didn't buy a ticket for the lottery.
6 _____ people _____ in houses in space in 2010?

I can make predictions about the future.

MY EVALUATION ☐☐☐☐

SPEAKING ● Making and responding to suggestions

6 Complete the dialogue with the words in the box.

> suggest   How   idea   going   can't
> Why   sure   matter   Let's

Luke What's the ¹_____, Rosa?
Rosa I think we're lost again!
Luke Oh no. What are we ²_____ to do?
Rosa ³_____ buy a map of the city.
Luke I'm not ⁴_____ about that. I can't see any shops near here.
Rosa ⁵_____ about asking that woman?
Luke We ⁶_____ do that. She's talking to her friend.
Rosa Well, what do you ⁷_____?
Luke ⁸_____ don't we find a bus or a taxi?
Rosa That's a good ⁹_____!

I can make and respond to suggestions.

MY EVALUATION ☐☐☐☐

WRITING ● A blog

7 Choose the correct answers to complete the blog.

Saturday 10th July

I'm going to go ¹_____ an expedition with my school next Friday. We're going to ²_____ at a big campsite in Snowdonia in Wales.

Saturday 17th July

³_____ I am next to my new tent. It's a really ⁴_____ day and I'm wearing my waterproof clothes.

Sunday 18th July

⁵_____ is me in my helmet. We climbed a big mountain this morning. I had a fantastic ⁶_____, but I was quite scared!

1 a on   b at   c in   d up
2 a take   b fall   c stay   d have
3 a This   b That   c Where   d Here
4 a rainy   b rain   c raining   d rained
5 a These   b This   c Those   d Where
6 a hour   b play   c time   d times

I can write a blog about an expedition.

MY EVALUATION ☐☐☐☐

Possessive 's

For singular nouns add 's to the noun.
the boy's room
For plural nouns add '.
the teachers' desk
For irregular plural nouns add 's.
the children's teacher
When there is more than one noun, add 's to the last noun only.
Jack and Lucy's mother

Use

The possessive 's shows that something belongs to a person.
Suzy's dictionary.   The girls' bags.

Subject pronouns and possessive adjectives

Subject pronouns	Possessive adjectives
I / you	my / your
he / she / it	his / her / its
we / you / they	our / your / their

Use

Subject pronouns are used in place of names or nouns.
The book is here. It is on the table.
Possessive adjectives show that something belongs to a person.
Paul's pencil is here. His pencil is on the desk.
Remember: Subject pronouns cannot be left out of a sentence.
She is in the classroom.   ~~Is in the classroom.~~

be: affirmative, negative and questions

Affirmative		Negative	
Full form	Short form	Full form	Short form
I am	I'm	I am not	I'm not
You are	You're	You are not	You aren't
He is	He's	He is not	He isn't
She is	She's	She is not	She isn't
It is	It's	It is not	It isn't
We are	We're	We are not	We aren't
You are	You're	You are not	You aren't
They are	They're	They are not	They aren't

The verb *be* follows the subject.
I am twelve years old.
The negative form is formed by adding *not* after the verb.
He is not in my class.
In spoken or informal written English it is common to use the short forms.
He isn't in my class.   You aren't at home.

Questions	Short answers	
	Affirmative	Negative
Am I ... ?	Yes, I am.	No, I'm not.
Are you ... ?	Yes, you are.	No, you aren't.
Is he ... ?	Yes, he is.	No, he isn't.
Is she ... ?	Yes, she is.	No, she isn't.
Is it ... ?	Yes, it is.	No, it isn't.
Are we ... ?	Yes, we are.	No, we aren't.
Are you ... ?	Yes, you are.	No, you aren't.
Are they ... ?	Yes, they are.	No, they aren't.

In yes / no questions reverse the position of the subject pronoun and the verb.
Are you popular at school?
Remember: There is no short form of affirmative short answers.

Use

The verb *be* is used to talk about the identity, description or place of a person, animal or object.
She is our teacher. Are you in Geneva? The bag isn't black.

Object pronouns

Subject pronoun	Object pronoun
I / you	me / you
he / she / it	him / her / it
we / you/ they	us / you / them

I'm next to Sam. I'm next to him.
Note that for things we use *it* (singular) or *them* (plural).
We're near the window. We're near it.
You're near the windows. You're near them.

Use

Object pronouns are used in place of names or nouns. We use them after verbs and prepositions.

Possessive 's

1 Rewrite the sentences adding 's or ' to the subjects.

The four girls desks.

The four girls' desks.

1 Maria book.

_____

2 Michael and Ruby classroom.

_____

3 The two boys dictionaries.

_____

4 Susan poster.

_____

5 Ben and Joe CD player.

_____

6 The students classroom.

_____

7 My two sisters books.

_____

8 Our friend house.

_____

Subject pronouns and possessive adjectives

2 Match the subject pronouns 1–7 with the possessive adjectives a–g.

1 I   a their
2 you   b his
3 he   c our
4 she   d its
5 it   e my
6 we   f your
7 they   g her

3 Complete the sentences. Put the words in brackets in the correct positions.

(your / I)   I'm in _your_ classroom.

1 (his / she) _____ is _____ friend.

2 (it / her) _____'s in _____ bag.

3 (you / my) _____ aren't _____ teacher!

4 (they / his) _____ mum and dad are teachers. _____'re in our school.

5 (your / I) _____'m not at _____ school.

6 (he / their) _____ dad is at home. _____'s a teacher.

be: affirmative, negative and questions

4 Complete the affirmative sentences using the correct form of be. Use short forms.

I'_m_ a teacher.

1 You_____ in my class.

2 He_____ near the door.

3 She_____ in the classroom.

4 It_____ on the desk.

5 We_____ in class 8S.

6 They_____ next to the laptop.

5 Rewrite the sentences in exercise 4 using the negative form.

I'm not a teacher.

1 _____

2 _____

3 _____

4 _____

5 _____

6 _____

6 Complete the questions and short answers.

_Am_ I in your class?   Yes, _you are_ .

1 _____ he my teacher?   No, _____.

2 _____ she on the chair?   Yes, _____.

3 _____ they nice?   No, _____.

4 _____ it under the desk?   Yes, _____.

5 _____ we near the school?   No, _____.

6 _____ you popular?   Yes, _____.

Object pronouns

7 Choose the correct words.

This is my bag. My pen is in **it** / **them**.

1 Freddie and Cara are in a new class. Dominic is with **her** / **them**.

2 I am in Berlin now. Mia is with **me** / **it**.

3 The teacher is in California today. We aren't with **her** / **you**.

4 Tony is next to the Simpsons poster. He's next to **it** / **him**.

5 You're near Gabriella and me. You're near **us** / **them**.

6 You and Joseph are in Vienna. Michael is with **you** / **her**.

7 John is my friend. I like **it** / **him**.

have got

Affirmative	Negative
I've got a pen.	I haven't got a pen.
You've got a pen.	You haven't got a pen.
He's got a pen.	He hasn't got a pen.
She's got a pen.	She hasn't got a pen.
It's got a pen.	It hasn't got a pen.
We've got a pen.	We haven't got a pen.
You've got a pen.	You haven't got a pen.
They've got a pen.	They haven't got a pen.

The affirmative form is made with *have got* or *has got* plus subject.
The negative form is made with *have not got* or *has not got* plus subject.
Note that in spoken and informal written English the short forms *'ve got*, *'s got*, *haven't got* and *hasn't got* are used.

Questions	Affirmative	Negative
Have I got a pen?	Yes, I have.	No, I haven't.
Have you got a pen?	Yes, you have.	No, you haven't.
Has he got a pen?	Yes, he has.	No, he hasn't.
Has she got a pen?	Yes, she has.	No, she hasn't.
Has it got a pen?	Yes, it has.	No, it hasn't.
Have we got a pen?	Yes, we have.	No, we haven't.
Have you got a pen?	Yes, you have.	No, you haven't.
Have they got a pen?	Yes, they have.	No, they haven't.

Questions are made with *Have / Has* plus subject plus *got*.
Short answers are made with *have* without *got*.
Yes, I have.
~~*Yes, I have got.*~~
Note that question and negative forms are not made with *do / does* or *don't / doesn't*.
Have you got a sister?
~~*Do you have got a sister?*~~
He hasn't got a bag.
~~*He doesn't have got a bag.*~~

Use
Have got is used to talk about possession. It is also used to talk about our families.
I've got a digital camera.
He hasn't got a pencil.
Have you got a brother? No, I haven't.

Prepositions: *about, of, by*

a book about tennis	a film about Africa
a photo of Rome	a poster of Orlando Bloom
a CD by Alicia Keys	a play by Shakespeare

Interrogative pronouns

Who's your favourite sports star?
Where's your friend from?
What's your favourite film?
When's your birthday?
How old is your cousin?
How many computer games have you got?
Use the interrogative pronouns *who*, *where*, *what*, *when*, *how old*, *how many* at the beginning of questions to ask about specific information.
Note that in informal and spoken English we often contract the verb *be* with question words *Who*, *Where*, *What*, *When* and *How old*.
Who's your favourite tennis player?
What's your name?
Where's your new school?

this, that, these, those

Singular	Plural
This is my friend Harry.	These are my friends James and Mia.
That's a good poster.	Those are cool T-shirts.

Use *this* and *these* for things that are close to the person who is speaking.
Use *that* and *those* for things that are further away from the person who is speaking.

have got

1 Write affirmative ✔ or negative ✗ sentences using *have got*. Use contractions where possible.

she / a book about animals ✔

She's got a book about animals.

1 I / a DVD player ✔

_____

2 he / a white rat ✗

_____

3 they / an English friend ✔

_____

4 you / a hip hop CD ✗

_____

5 Natasha / a red football shirt ✔

_____

6 I / a blue pen ✗

_____

2 Look at the information in the table and write questions and short answers using *have got*.

	Jasmine	Jack and Ella
a dog	✗	✓
a new teacher	✓	✗
a blue pen	✗	✓
computer	✓	✗

Has Jasmine got a dog?

No, she hasn't.

1 _____
_____

2 _____
_____

3 _____
_____

4 _____
_____

5 _____
_____

6 _____
_____

7 _____
_____

Prepositions: *about, of, by*

3 Complete the sentences with *about, of* or *by*.

Have you got a CD _____ **by** _____ Rihanna?

1 Paula is interested in books _____ animals.

2 I haven't got a photo _____ my cat.

3 I like the new CD _____ Kanye West.

4 Have they got a poster _____ the football team?

5 We're into books and magazines _____ photography.

6 Has she got a nice photo _____ her family?

Interrogative pronouns

4 Complete the interrogative pronouns.

W**ho's** your favourite tennis player?

1 H_____ are your cousins?

2 W_____'s your favourite TV programme?

3 W_____ 's your mobile phone?

4 H_____ books have you got?

5 W_____ 's your sister's birthday?

6 W_____ are those boys?

5 Match answers a–f with questions 1–6 in exercise 4.

a It's *The X Factor*. [2]

b On 17th May. ☐

c They're my brothers. ☐

d Two or three hundred! ☐

e They're twelve and fifteen. ☐

f It's in my bag. ☐

this, that, these, those

6 Choose the correct words.

(This) / These is my best friend, Sara.

1 **This / These** are my cousins, Joshua and Emily.

2 Is your food good? Yes, **this / these** pizza is fantastic!

3 Look. **That / Those** DVDs are very expensive.

4 **That / Those** girl is in my English class.

5 Hey, **that / those** shoes are cool.

6 Happy Birthday! **This / These** book is for you.

there is, there are + a, an, some and any

	Affirmative	Short form
Singular	There is a / an ...	There's a / an ...
Plural	There are some ...	–

There is is used with *a / an* and singular nouns and *there are* with plural nouns.
There is a school.
There's an art gallery.
There are some books on the table.
Note that in spoken and informal written English the short form *there's* is used. *There are* does not have a short form.

	Negative	Short form
Singular	There is not a / an ...	There isn't a / an ...
Plural	There are not any ...	There aren't any ...

The negative form *there is not* is used with singular nouns and *there are not* with plural nouns.
Note that in spoken and informal written English the short form *there isn't* and *there aren't* are used. *Any* is used with plural nouns.
There isn't a sports centre near here.
There aren't any chairs in the library.

Use

There is / there are is used to express the existence or absence of someone or something.
There's a river near my school.
There are some cars in the car park.
There aren't any big shops in this town.

Is there ...?, Are there ...?

Questions	Short answers	
	Affirmative	Negative
Is there a / an ... ?	Yes, there is.	No, there isn't.
Are there any ... ?	Yes, there are.	No, there aren't.
How many ... are there?	Four.	

The question form *Is there* is used with *a / an* and a singular noun.
Is there a cinema in your town?
Is there an email for me?

The plural form *Are there* is used with *any* and a plural noun.
Are there any shops?
How many .... are there? is used when asking about a specific number of people or things.
How many parks are there? (There are) two.
In negative short answers it is common to use the short form *isn't* and *aren't*.
No, it isn't.   **No, there aren't.**

Comparative adjectives

Most adjectives with one syllable add -er	clean – cleaner
One syllable with one vowel ending with one consonant double consonant and add -er	big – bigger
One syllable ending in -e add -r	safe – safer
Irregular	good – better bad – worse
Adjectives ending in -y leave out -y, and add -ier	pretty – prettier
All other adjectives of two or more syllables put more before adjective	expensive – more expensive

Use

Comparative adjectives are used to compare things, places or people. The comparative adjectives is followed by *than*.
Libraries are quieter than schools.
My flat is nicer than your flat.

Prepositions: by and on

	by	on
I go to work ...	by bus.	on the bus.
She goes to London ...	by coach.	on the coach.
He goes to the office ...	by train.	on the train.
I go to Spain ...	by plane.	on the plane.
The café is ten minutes ...	by car.	–
They go to the shops ...	–	on foot.

there is, there are + a, an, some and any

1 Complete the affirmative ✓ and negative ✗ sentences with *is*, *are*, *isn't* and *aren't*.

There _____*is*_____ a table. ✓

1 There _____ two boys. ✓
2 There _____ a cinema. ✗
3 There _____ some books. ✓
4 There _____ any flats near here. ✗
5 There _____ an art gallery. ✓
6 There _____ a park. ✗
7 There _____ any factories. ✗
8 There _____ some animals. ✓

2 Complete the sentences with *a*, *an*, *some* or *any*.

There isn't _____*a*_____ cinema.

1 There's _____ email.
2 There are _____ CDs.
3 There's _____ window.
4 There aren't _____ pencils.
5 There are _____ shelves.
6 There isn't _____ a shopping centre.
7 There aren't _____ posters.
8 There's _____ office.

Is there ...?, Are there ...?

3 Complete the questions and answers using the words in the box. Use the words more than once.

```
are   aren't   how   is   two   there's
many   there   isn't
```

__*Is*__ there a book?
No, there __*isn't.*__

1 _____ there any shops?
  Yes, there _____.
2 _____ there an email?
  No, there _____.
3 _____ there any parks?
  No, there _____.
4 _____ many flats are there?
  There are _____.
5 _____ there a shopping centre?
  Yes, there _____.
6 How _____ sports centres are _____?
  _____ one.

Comparative adjectives

4 Write the comparative adjectives.

small   __*smaller*__

1 pretty   _____
2 difficult   _____
3 fast   _____
4 bad   _____
5 expensive   _____
6 easy   _____
7 interesting   _____
8 far   _____
9 ugly   _____
10 exciting   _____

5 Complete the sentences with the comparative form of the adjectives in brackets and *than*.

He's __*older than*__ (old) me.

1 Football is _____ (popular) tennis.
2 My bag is _____ (nice) your bag.
3 The library is _____ (big) the school.
4 DVD players are _____ (cheap) TVs.
5 Jack is _____ (friendly) Tom.
6 My laptop is _____ (good) my computer.
7 Skiing is _____ (dangerous) chess.
8 Canada is _____ (cold) Spain.
9 Her bike is _____ (expensive) your bike.
10 I think Rome is _____ (beautiful) Paris.

Prepositions: *by* and *on*

6 Complete the sentences with *by* or *on*.

I go to school __*by*__ bus.

1 She travels to work _____ the train.
2 The office is about ten minutes _____ foot.
3 Adam goes to school _____ car.
4 We go to Paris _____ the plane.
5 It's about two hours to London _____ train.
6 Mark goes to London _____ the coach.

Present simple: affirmative and negative

Affirmative	Negative
I speak French.	I don't speak French.
You speak French.	You don't speak French.
He speaks French.	He doesn't speak French.
She speaks French.	She doesn't speak French.
It speaks French.	It doesn't speak French.
We speak French.	We don't speak French.
You speak French.	You don't speak French.
They speak French.	They don't speak French.

The affirmative form is the base form of the verb (infinitive without *to*). To make the third person singular (*he / she / it*) add *-s* or *-es*; for verbs ending in *-y*, delete *-y* and add *-ies*.

I live	he lives
you go	she goes
we try	he tries

The negative form is made with *do not* or *does not* plus the base form of the verb.

Note that in spoken and informal written English the short forms *don't* or *doesn't* are used.

I don't eat pizza. *She doesn't eat pizza.*

Present simple: questions

Questions	Short answers	
	Affirmative	Negative
Do I speak Italian?	Yes, I do.	No, I don't.
Do you speak Italian?	Yes, you do.	No, you don't.
Does he speak Italian?	Yes, he does.	No, he doesn't.
Does she speak Italian?	Yes, she does.	No, she doesn't.
Does it speak Italian?	Yes, it does.	No, it doesn't.
Do we speak Italian?	Yes, we do.	No, we don't.
Do you speak Italian?	Yes, you do.	No, you don't.
Do they speak Italian?	Yes, they do.	No, they don't.

Do they speak Italian? *Yes, they do.*
Do you speak Italian? *No, we don't.*

The question form is made with *Do* or *Does* + subject + verb.

Short answers are made with *do* or *does* in the affirmative and *don't* or *doesn't* in the negative.

Question word	Auxiliary verb	Subject	Verb
What	does	she	eat?
Where	do	you	live?
When	does	Kevin	get up?
Who	do	they	visit?
What time	does	the lesson	start?
How often	do	you	read?

Put question words at the beginning of the question.

Where does he work?

Remember to include the auxiliary verb *do / does* in questions.

Where do you live? ~~Where you live?~~

Use

The present simple is used:

1 to talk and ask questions about habits, routines and things that happen regularly.
   She goes to school at nine o'clock.
2 to describe things that are always true, or almost always true.
   I live in Warsaw. *My teacher doesn't speak Polish.*
3 to talk about what we think, feel or like.
   Do you like Turkish music?

Adverbs of frequency

always	●●●●●
usually	●●●●○
often	●●●○○
sometimes	●●○○○
never	○○○○○

In sentences with *be*, adverbs of frequency follow the verb *be*.

I am always friendly.

However, with all other verbs, adverbs of frequency precede the verb.

I often get up at 6.00.

In questions, adverbs of frequency always follow the subject.

Do you usually watch TV?
Are your friends always noisy?

Use

Adverbs of frequency are used to describe how often you do something.

Present simple: affirmative and negative

1 Complete the sentences using the present simple affirmative form of the verbs in brackets.

We _____use_____ (use) dictionaries in class.

1 David _____ (watch) American DVDs.
2 My friend's father _____ (teach) Italian.
3 Carla _____ (study) English after school.
4 I _____ (live) near the school.
5 My sister _____ (like) cats and dogs.
6 They _____ (speak) Japanese at home.

2 Complete the sentences using the negative form of the verbs in bold.

My friend **watches** TV programmes, but he _doesn't watch_ **films**.

1 Justin and Charlie **play** basketball, but they _____ tennis.
2 My sister **speaks** English, but she _____ German.
3 You **read** books, but you _____ comics.
4 Clara **goes** to the library, but she _____ to the park.
5 We **like** hip hop music, but we _____ classical music.
6 Mr Holmes **teaches** Italian, but he _____ French.
7 I **use** a dictionary, but I _____ a grammar book.
8 I **write** emails, but I _____ letters.

Present simple: questions

3 Order the words to make questions. Then complete the short answers.

you / food / like / do / French
Do you like French food?

Yes, _____I do._____

1 father / your / Japanese / speak / does
_____
No, _____.
2 they / a / do / go / school / language / to
_____
Yes, _____.
3 live / he / near / does / hospital / the
_____
Yes, _____.

4 understand / you / this / do / word
_____
No, _____.
5 Anna / does / DVDs / English / watch / in
_____
Yes, _____.
6 they / do / in / factory / work / a
_____
No, _____.

4 Look at the answers. Then write the questions.

Where _____ _do you live_ _____?
I live near the train station.

1 What films _____?
I like French films.
2 Where _____?
He works in the art gallery.
3 What time _____?
She gets up at 6.30.
4 How _____?
They travel to school by bus.
5 How often _____?
He plays basketball every day.
6 When _____?
I finish work at 4.30.

Adverbs of frequency

5 Look at the key. Write sentences with the correct adverb of frequency.

always	●●●●●
usually	●●●●○
often	●●●○○
sometimes	●●○○○
never	○○○○○

I do my homework. ●●●●●
I always do my homework.

1 He has lunch at work. ●●●●
_____
2 They finish work after 5.00. ●●
_____
3 The dog is dirty. ●●●●●
_____
4 He gets up early. ●●●
_____
5 She goes to bed at 8.30. ○○○○○
_____

Present continuous: affirmative and negative

Affirmative		Negative	
I'm	running.	I'm not	running.
You're	running.	You aren't	running.
He's	running.	He isn't	running.
She's	running.	She isn't	running.
It's	running.	It isn't	running.
We're	running.	We aren't	running.
You're	running.	You aren't	running.
They're	running.	They aren't	running.

The affirmative form of the present continuous is made with the verb *be* and the *-ing* form of the verb.

She's walking to school.

The negative form is made with the verb *be* + *not* and the *-ing* form.

Note that in spoken and informal written English, short forms are used.

They aren't eating.

Spelling rules

With the majority of verbs add *-ing*.

eat → eating   think → thinking

With verbs that end in *-e* delete *e* and add *-ing*.

have → having   write → writing

With verbs that end in vowel + single consonant double the consonant and add *-ing*.

stop → stopping   swim → swimming

Present continuous: questions

Question	Short answers	
	Affirmative	Negative
Am I playing?	Yes, I am.	No, I'm not.
Are you playing?	Yes, you are.	No, you aren't.
Is he playing?	Yes, he is.	No, he isn't.
Is she playing?	Yes, she is.	No, she isn't.
Is it playing?	Yes, it is.	No, it isn't.
Are we playing?	Yes, we are.	No, we aren't.
Are you playing?	Yes, you are.	No, you aren't.
Are they playing?	Yes, they are.	No, they aren't.

The question form is made by inverting the verb *be* and the subject.

Are you playing football?

What are you reading?

Short answers are made with the verb *be* only, without the *-ing* form.

Are you doing your homework? Yes, I am.

Are they building a new house? No, they aren't.

Present continuous and present simple

Use

The present continuous is used to talk about actions in progress.

She's playing tennis now.

They're watching a film on TV at the moment.

The present simple is used to talk about routines or repeated actions.

He plays tennis every weekend.

We watch The Simpsons **every evening.**

Note that there are some verbs (stative verbs) which are not usually used in the continuous form. These include: *understand, know, think, like, love, hate* and *want*.

I like that CD.

~~**I'm liking that CD.**~~

Present continuous: affirmative and negative

1 Write the *-ing* form of the verbs.

look   _looking_

1 run   _____
2 attack   _____
3 play   _____
4 sit   _____
5 swim   _____
6 practise   _____
7 eat   _____
8 change   _____
9 catch   _____
10 hide   _____

2 Complete the sentences using the present continuous form of the verbs in brackets.

My friends ____ _are chatting_ ____ (chat) on the internet.

1 Sofia _____ (write) an email to her cousin.
2 You _____ (not listen) to the radio.
3 We _____ (watch) an interesting programme on TV.
4 Diego _____ (talk) to his father on the phone.
5 I _____ (not do) my homework on the computer.
6 They _____ (not use) that Spanish dictionary.
7 Rob and Angela _____ (swim) at the moment.
8 The shark _____ (look for) food.

Present continuous: questions

3 Complete the questions and short answers.

____ _Is_ ____ she listening? Yes, ___ _she is ._ ___

1 _____ he making dinner?
  No, _____.
2 _____ they reading comics?
  Yes, _____.
3 _____ we studying science?
  Yes, _____.
4 _____ she eating pizza?
  Yes, _____.

5 _____ you watching that film?
  No, _____.
6 _____ it feeding its babies?
  Yes, _____.

4 Complete the questions.

A I'm making dinner.
B What _____ _are you making_ _____?

1 A She's studying in her bedroom.
  B What _____?
2 A The frog is hiding from the snake.
  B Where _____?
3 A My sister is teaching English.
  B Who _____?
4 A They're watching TV.
  B What _____?
5 A The elephants are running to the river.
  B Where _____?
6 A Daniel is playing a computer game.
  B What _____?

Present continuous and present simple

5 Complete the sentences using the present continuous or the present simple form of the verbs in brackets.

I ____ _meet_ ____ (meet) my friends every day after school.

1 Anna _____ (swim) in the pool every day.
2 Where are John and Rob?
  They _____ (play) tennis at the moment.
3 My parents _____ (make) dinner at seven o'clock every evening.
4 Naomi _____ (watch) a DVD now.
5 Ben _____ (speak) Italian and German.
6 Where's Becky?
  She _____ (read) a book in her bedroom.
7 Mum isn't here. She _____ (run) in the park.
8 We usually _____ (have) lunch at home.
9 I _____ (play) the piano after school every day.
10 Mike and Jamie are in their room. They _____ (do) their homework.

can for ability and permission

The affirmative form is made with the subject plus *can* plus the base form.

I can dance.

They can have a pizza.

The negative form is made with the subject plus *can't* (*cannot*) plus the base form.

In spoken and informal written English it is common to use the short form *can't*.

She can't swim.

We can't speak German.

Questions are made with *can* plus the subject plus the base form.

Can Sarah have dinner here?

Can you speak Polish?

Remember: Always use the base form of the verb with *can*, not the full infinitive.

I can play the guitar.

~~I can to play the guitar.~~

Can she listen to your CD?

~~Can she to listen to your CD?~~

Remember: Never use the auxiliary verb *do* / *does* in questions with *can*.

Can I have some sweets?

~~Do I can have some sweets?~~

Use

Can is used to express permission and ability.

Permission
Can I have some chips?
Yes, you can.
Can we go to the cinema?
No, we can't.
Ability
I can do martial arts.
Can he speak German?

Countable and uncountable nouns: *a / an, the, some, any, much, many* and *a lot of*

Countable nouns have a singular and a plural form:

apple   apples

Use (*a / an*) with singular countable nouns.

a banana   an apple

Use *the* with both singular and plural nouns.

the shop   the shops

Countable nouns have a plural form.

The apple is on the table.   The apples are on the table.

Uncountable nouns don't have a plural form.

The pasta is very nice.   ~~The pasta are very nice.~~

Use *the* or no article with uncountable nouns. Don't use *a /an* or numbers.

fruit	meat	the water	the rice
~~a fruit~~	~~a meat~~	~~two fruits~~	~~three meats~~

Use *a / an* when we talk about something for the first time. Use *the* when we mention it a second time.

I've got an apple in my bag. The apple is green.

Use *the* when there is only one thing:

What is the capital of your country?

I eat in the school canteen.

Some, any and *a lot of* can be used with plural countable nouns and uncountable nouns.

Some is used in affirmative sentences and indicates an undefined amount of something:

I've got some apples.

There's some ice cream on the table.

A lot of is used in affirmative sentences and indicates a large quantity of something.

There are a lot of frogs here.   There is a lot of salad.

Any is used in negative sentences and questions.

There aren't any chairs.

There isn't any water.   Is there any cheese?

Much is used in negative sentences with uncountable nouns.

There isn't much pasta.

Many is used in negative sentences with plural countable nouns.

There aren't many burgers.

Not much and *not many* indicate a small amount of something.

There isn't much milk.

There aren't many apples.

can for ability and permission

1 Write questions and short answers.

	Jake	Mia and Georgia
swim	✗	✓
speak French	✓	✗
play the piano	✗	✓
cook	✓	✗

Jake / swim / ?

Can Jake swim?   *No, he can't.*

1 Mia and Georgia / play the piano / ?

_____

_____

2 Jake / speak French / ?

_____

_____

3 Mia and Georgia / swim / ?

_____

_____

4 Jake / cook / ?

_____

_____

5 Mia and Georgia / speak French / ?

_____

_____

6 Jake / play the piano / ?

_____

_____

7 Mia and Georgia / cook / ?

_____

_____

2 Complete the sentences and questions with *can / can't* and the verbs in the box.

> learn   not drink   go   not watch   stay
> make   ~~buy~~

____Can____ we ____buy____ a dog?

1 _____ I _____ to bed at 11.30?

2 _____ you _____ Italian?

3 Sorry, you _____ that horror film.

4 My friend _____ at our house tonight!

5 _____ I _____ a big chocolate cake?

6 We _____ the orange juice.

Countable and uncountable nouns: *a / an, the, some, any, much, many* and *a lot of*

3 Complete the table.

> ~~egg~~   restaurant   air   pen   music
> food   chair   time   book

Countable	Uncountable
____egg____	_____
_____	_____
_____	_____
_____	

4 Complete the sentences with *a, an, some* or *any*.

There are ____some____ vegetables on the table.

1 I'm eating _____ sandwich.

2 Are there _____ sweets?

3 There aren't _____ burgers.

4 I've got _____ pasta for lunch.

5 My dad eats _____ egg every morning.

6 We've got _____ rice with beans.

5 Complete the sentences with *much, many* or *a lot of*.

Sally doesn't drink ____much____ water.

1 There aren't _____ chairs in the classroom.

2 There isn't _____ fruit in Tony's diet.

3 Jack eats _____ meat.

4 I haven't got _____ sweets in my bag.

5 Mum always makes _____ pasta for dinner.

6 I'm sorry. There isn't _____ milk.

6 Complete the sentences with *a, an* or *the*.

I often go to __the__ big park next to our school.

1 Here's _____ sandwich and some crisps. _____ sandwich has got meat in it.

2 What's _____ name of your dog?

3 Every day I eat _____ apple and _____ pear.

4 I'm chatting to _____ friend.

5 Where is _____ cinema in this town?

6 He usually has _____ fizzy drink after school.

was, were

Affirmative	Negative
I was happy.	I wasn't happy.
You were happy.	You weren't happy.
He / She / It was happy.	He / She / It wasn't happy.
We / You / They were happy.	We / You / They weren't happy.

The past simple affirmative form of the verb *be* is *was* or *were*.

The past simple negative form is *was not* or *were not*. Note that the contractions *wasn't* or *weren't* are usually used.

Question	Short answers	
	Affirmative	Negative
Was I at school?	Yes, I was.	No, I wasn't.
Were you at school?	Yes, you were.	No, you weren't.
Was he / she / it at school?	Yes, he / she / it was.	No, he / she / it wasn't.
Were we / you / they at school?	Yes, we / you / they were.	No, we / you / they weren't.

The question form is made with *was* or *were* plus subject.

Short answers are made with *Yes* or *No* plus subject plus *was*, *were*, *wasn't* or *weren't*.

there was, there were

There was and *there were* are the past simple forms of *there is* and *there are*.

There was an old house here ten years ago.
There were 24 children in the class last year.

Past simple of regular verbs: affirmative and negative

Affirmative	Negative
I listened.	I didn't listen.
You listened.	You didn't listen.
He / She / It listened.	He / She / It didn't listen.
We / You / They listened.	We / You / They didn't listen.

The affirmative form of past simple regular verbs is made by adding *-ed* to the base form of the verb. The negative form is made with *did not* plus the base form. The contraction *didn't* is usually used.

Use

The past simple is used to talk about finished actions in the past and actions which happen at a specific time.

I played tennis two hours ago.
We didn't visit London last year.

Spelling rules: past simple affirmative

With the majority of verbs add *-ed*.

watch → watched   check → checked

With verbs that end in *-e* add *-d*.

like → liked   live → lived

With verbs that end in a vowel + single consonant double the consonant and add *-ed*.

stop → stopped   travel → travelled

Past time expressions

The past simple can be used with a number of time expressions:

last week / month / year / weekend / Sunday
in the 17th century
in 1964 / May 1865
yesterday
three days / two weeks / 300 years ago

The time expressions usually go at the end of a sentence or phrase, but they can also go at the beginning.

We travelled to China last year.
Last year we travelled to China.

was, were

1 Complete the sentences with *was, wasn't, were* or *weren't.*

Van Gogh wasn't a writer. He ____was____ an artist.

1 They _____ at the match. They were on holiday.
2 It wasn't hot in France. It _____ very cold.
3 I _____ at school yesterday. I was at home.
4 We weren't at the park. We _____ at the cinema.
5 That bag wasn't cheap. It _____ expensive.
6 You _____ at the cinema. You were in the park.

2 Write questions with *was* or *were*. Then write short answers.

your sister / at the party / last night / ? (Yes)
<u>Was your sister at the party last night?</u>
<u>Yes, she was.</u>

1 they / at the station / at three o'clock / ? (No)
_____
_____

2 your brother / in the football team / last year / ? (Yes)
_____
_____

3 you / on holiday / last week / ? (No)
_____
_____

4 the water / in the swimming pool / cold / ? (Yes)
_____
_____

there was, there were

3 Complete the sentences using the affirmative or negative form of *there was* or *there were.*

In 1830, _there weren't_ any cars on the roads.

1 In the 1800s _____ any computers.
2 In 1850 _____ a lot of horses on the roads.
3 _____ an airport here 200 years ago.
4 _____ any MP3 players 20 years ago.
5 _____ a brilliant actor in that film about Columbus.

Past simple of regular verbs: affirmative and negative

4 Complete the sentences using the past simple form of the words in the box.

> change   listen   travel   live   name
> play   ~~visit~~

When we were in Paris we ___visited___ the Eiffel Tower and the Louvre museum.

1 She _____ her cat after a footballer.
2 That singer _____ his name to Blake.
3 He _____ football last night.
4 She _____ in a big house in Paris.
5 I _____ to some cool music yesterday.
6 We _____ to Brazil six months ago.

5 Rewrite the sentences in the negative form.

My sister liked that new CD.
<u>My sister didn't like that new CD.</u>

1 They used a dictionary in class.
_____
2 John stayed at Peter's house last night.
_____
3 Maria visited her friend yesterday.
_____
4 You changed school last year.
_____
5 Einstein invented the computer.
_____
6 I chatted to my friend on the phone.
_____

Past time expressions

6 Choose the correct answers.

We watched a film _____ Saturday.
a at   (b last)   c in   d ago

1 I visited the art gallery two weeks _____.
  a last   b now   c ago   d time
2 We finished our homework _____ night.
  a last   b in   c ago   d on
3 People didn't travel by car _____ 1780.
  a at   b in   c on   d of
4 We were at the shopping centre _____.
  a later   b now   c ago   d yesterday
5 Columbus discovered America _____ 1492.
  a last   b at   c in   d on

Past simple: regular and irregular verbs

Subject	Affirmative	Negative
I	had.	didn't have.
You	practised.	didn't practise.
He / She / It	built.	didn't build.
We / You / They	used.	didn't use.

The past simple has only one form for all persons of the verb.

I went shopping.

She went shopping.

We went shopping.

Regular verbs add -*ed* to the base form.

play → played   visit → visited   look → looked

Verbs ending in -*e* add -*d*.

live → lived   share → shared   chase → chased

Irregular verbs each have their own past simple form.

buy → bought   go → went   have → had   meet → met

run → ran   see → saw   win → won   write → wrote

The negative form is made with *didn't* plus the base form.

She didn't meet her friend.

We didn't play the video game.

Remember: Don't use *didn't* with the verb *be*.

The flat wasn't very big.

They weren't interested in sport.

Past simple: questions

Auxiliary verb	Subject	Verb
Did	I	see?
	you	play?
	he / she / it	dance?
	we / you / they	eat?

The question form is made with the auxiliary verb *did* plus the base form.

Did you have dinner at home?

Did he win the race?

Did she design the game?

Did they do the homework?

Question word	Auxiliary verb	Subject	Verb
What			
When		I	go?
Where	did	you	get up?
Who		he / she / it	visit?
How often		we / you / they	buy?
What time			

Wh- words go at the beginning of questions.

When did she have lunch?

Who did we see in the park?

Remember: Don't use *did* in questions with *be*.

Was she good at tennis?

Were you at the cinema yesterday?

Short answers are formed with the auxiliary verb only.

Did you see the film?   *Yes, we did.*

Did she like this book?   *No, she didn't.*

Use

Use the past simple to describe events which happened at a specific point in the past. For this reason sentences in the simple past often include a time phrase such as:

yesterday, in 2002, three weeks ago, last year.

I saw him ten minutes ago.

We went swimming yesterday.

They visited me in 2004.

He won the race last year.

Past simple: regular and irregular verbs

1 Write the past simple form of the verbs in the correct columns.

	-d	-ed	irregular
eat			ate
play			
find			
use			
visit			
like			
buy			
ask			
lose			

2 Write past simple sentences.

he / not go / to the shopping centre

He didn't go to the shopping centre.

1 she / win / a laptop

_____

2 they / eat / some burgers

_____

3 I / buy / some sweets

_____

4 he / not see / me

_____

5 we / not like / the film

_____

6 I / make / dinner / last night

_____

3 Rewrite the sentences using the past simple.

You work in a sports centre.

You worked in a sports centre.

1 We travel to school by bus.

_____

2 She buys a lot of clothes.

_____

3 He plays volleyball in the afternoon.

_____

4 I visit my friends in France.

_____

5 She meets us at the park.

_____

6 They go to school by bus.

_____

Past simple: questions

4 Write past simple questions. Then complete the short answers.

you / watch / the film / last night / ?

Did you watch the film last night?

Yes, I _____did_____.

1 she / break / the swimming record / ?

_____

No, she _____.

2 he / beat / his friend / at table tennis / ?

_____

Yes, he _____.

3 you / design / this new game / ?

_____

Yes, I _____.

4 they / have / a barbecue / yesterday / ?

_____

No, they _____.

5 Complete the dialogue using past simple questions. Use the words in the box.

> stay do come get up see take eat

Tom	What did you _____do_____ at the weekend?
Sophie	I went to Amsterdam with my family.
Tom	Really? Where [1] _____?
Sophie	In a hotel near the airport.
Tom	What [2] _____?
Sophie	All the important places. We saw the Anne Frank house and the Van Gogh museum.
Tom	Cool. [3] _____ any nice photos?
Sophie	Yes, I did. I took photos on my phone.
Tom	And where [4] _____?
Sophie	In a great restaurant near our hotel.
Tom	When [5] _____ home?
Sophie	Late on Sunday evening.
Tom	[6] _____ early on Monday?
Sophie	No, I didn't. I was very tired!

Imperatives

Affirmative	Negative
Look.	Don't look.
Close the window.	Don't close the window.
Be quiet.	Don't be noisy.

The imperative form is the base form of the verb. The negative form of the imperative is made with *don't* and the base form.

Don't look now! There's a big spider over there!

Use

The affirmative form of the imperative is used to give instructions or orders.

Sit down.

Open your books.

Read this page.

The negative form of the imperative is used to express prohibition.

Don't talk.

Don't watch TV.

Don't eat that biscuit.

be going to

Affirmative	Negative
I'm going to win.	I'm not going to win.
You're going to win.	You aren't going to win.
He's going to win.	He isn't going to win.
She's going to win.	She isn't going to win.
It's going to win.	It isn't going to win.
We're going to win.	We aren't going to win.
You're going to win.	You aren't going to win.
They're going to win.	They aren't going to win.

The affirmative form is made with the verb *be* and *going to* plus the base form.

We're going to have a coffee.

The negative form is made with the negative form of the verb *be* and *going to* plus the base form.

They aren't going to have lunch.

Note that in spoken and informal written English short forms are used.

Question	Short answers	
	Affirmative	Negative
Am I going to help?	Yes, I am.	No, I'm not.
Are you going to help?	Yes, you are.	No, you aren't.
Is he going to help?	Yes, he is.	No, he isn't.
Is she going to help?	Yes, she is.	No, she isn't.
Is it going to help?	Yes, it is.	No, it isn't.
Are we going to help?	Yes, we are.	No, we aren't.
Are you going to help?	Yes, you are.	No, you aren't.
Are they going to help?	Yes, they are.	No, they aren't.

The question form is made with the inverted form of the verb *be* and *going to* plus the base form.

Is she going to go to Spain?

Short answers are made only with the verb *be* without *going to*.

Are you going to play tennis?   **Yes, I am.**

Use

Be going to is used to talk about plans, intentions and things we have decided to do in the future.

will and won't

Affirmative
I / You / He / She / It / We / You / They will run.

Negative
I / You / He / She / It / We / You / They won't go.

Questions	Short answers	
	Affirmative	Negative
Will I / you / he / she / it / we / you / they stay?	Yes, I / you / he / she / it / we / you / they will.	No, I / you / he / she / it / we / you / they won't.

The affirmative form is made with *will* plus the base form.

The weather will be hotter in the future.

The negative form is made with *won't* plus the base form.

They won't win the volleyball match.

The question form is made with *will* plus subject plus the base form.

Will people live in houses in 2050?   **Where will they work?**

Use

Will is used to talk about future predictions.

Imperatives

1 Complete the sentences using affirmative or negative imperatives and the words in the box.

> drink   swim   ~~arrive~~   take   touch
> use   wear

_____Arrive_____ early at the airport – it's always a good idea.

1 _____ your passport – it's very important!

2 _____ sunscreen every day – it's always hot and sunny.

3 _____ insects in the jungle – some are dangerous.

4 _____ your torch at night – it's very dark in the rainforest.

5 _____ water from the river – it isn't a good idea.

6 _____ in the river – there are snakes in it!

be going to

2 Complete the sentences using the affirmative and negative form of *be going to* and the words in the box.

> eat   not help   discover   not play   revise
> travel   not wear   ~~watch~~   buy

He _'s going to watch_ Cristiano Ronaldo on TV.

1 They _____ pizza for dinner this evening.

2 I _____ basketball with Yusuf tomorrow.

3 You _____ me with my homework!

4 Helena _____ to Brazil by plane.

5 We _____ a new species of animal in the rainforest.

6 I _____ for the exam next week.

7 She _____ the new Harry Potter DVD.

8 He _____ that old T-shirt.

3 Jane, Hugo and Isaac are going to Scotland in August. Write questions and short answers.

	Jane	Hugo	Isaac
travel by train	✓	✗	✓
stay in a tent	✗	✗	✓
visit Loch Ness	✓	✗	✗

Hugo / travel by train / ?

Is Hugo going to travel by train? No, he isn't.

1 Jane and Isaac / travel by train / ?

_____

_____

2 Jane / stay in a tent / ?

_____

_____

3 Isaac / stay in a tent / ?

_____

_____

4 Hugo and Isaac / visit Loch Ness / ?

_____

_____

5 Jane / visit Loch Ness / ?

_____

_____

will and won't

4 Order the words to make sentences and questions.

extinct / tigers / become / will / future / the / in

Tigers will become extinct in the future.

1 travel / by / people / train / will

_____

2 weather / be / hotter / will / the

_____

3 live / won't / we / a / in / house / big

_____

4 at / use / won't / books / children / school

_____

_____

5 go / I / will / university / to / ?

_____

6 bears / polar / live / will / Arctic / the / in / ?

_____

_____

PRONUNCIATION BANK

Unit 1: Syllables

1 🔊 1.02 **How many syllables are in each word? Write the words in the correct list. Then listen and check.**

> ~~animals~~ ~~comics~~ sport ~~art~~ friends
> watching basketball music chatting
> books internet pen

one syllable	two syllables	three syllables
art	comics	animals
Exercise 2	Exercise 2	Exercise 2

2 🔊 1.03 **Read the words and add them to the table in exercise 1. Then listen and check.**

> difficult window nice poster
> expensive table door clock computer

3 **Read the words and write the number of syllables.**

1 notebook _____
2 cycling _____
3 bag _____
4 horrible _____
5 popular _____
6 American _____
7 small _____
8 photography _____

4 **Write two new words for each group.**

1 one syllable
good _____
2 two syllable
teacher _____
3 three syllable
important _____

Unit 2: /ə/

1 🔊 1.04 **Listen to the sound /ə/ in the words.**

1 bigger   4 older
2 computer   5 internet
3 centre   6 better

2 🔊 1.05 **Listen to the words and underline the sound /ə/.**

1 player   5 prettier
2 friendlier   6 printer
3 actor   7 horror
4 noisier   8 teacher

3 **Choose the word with an /ə/ sound. Then underline the /ə/ sound.**

1 There's a tall **building / skyscraper** in Dubai.
2 It's an **amazing / fantastic** place.
3 The lifts in the **tower / offices** are fast.
4 A lot of **visitors / people** like the tower.
5 There's a good visitor **area / café**.
6 It's open on **Sundays / Saturdays**.

4 **Choose a word in each group which doesn't have the /ə/ sound.**

1 poster	camera	photo	ruler
2 director	singer	drummer	guitar
3 faster	worse	cheaper	easier
4 park	river	gallery	weather
5 Canada	Australia	Poland	USA
6 near	between	under	about

Unit 3: Third person singular

1 🔊 1.06 **Listen to the sentences. Which verb form do you hear in each sentence? Tick ✓ A or B.**

	A	B
1	like	likes
2	go	goes
3	practise	practises
4	speak	speaks
5	know	knows
6	teach	teaches
7	write	writes
8	read	reads
9	use	uses

PRONUNCIATION BANK

2 🔊 1.07 Listen to the verbs from list B in exercise 1 and repeat. Which ending do you hear for each verb? Write the verbs in the correct list.

/s/	/z/	/ɪz/
likes		

3 Practise saying these sentences. Pay attention to the pronunciation of the verbs.

1 She teaches French and German.
2 He likes basketball and tennis.
3 She knows the answer.
4 He uses a computer.
5 She writes letters.
6 He goes to school every day.

4 Choose a verb in each group with the /ɪz/ sound.

1	watches	eats	reads	likes
2	visits	lives	finishes	works
3	travels	washes	does	walks
4	sleeps	has	gets	misses
5	plays	comes	mixes	buys

Unit 4: *-ing* /ɪŋ/

1 🔊 1.08 Listen and repeat the verbs. Pay attention to the /ɪŋ/ sound.

1 watching 5 jumping
2 hiding 6 running
3 eating 7 swimming
4 hunting 8 sleeping

2 🔊 1.09 Listen and repeat the questions.

1 What are you watching?
2 Where are you running?
3 What's he eating?
4 Why are you hiding?
5 What are they doing?

3 Practise saying the pairs of words.

1 play / playing 4 dig / digging
2 help / helping 5 get / getting
3 talk / talking 6 walk / walking

4 Practise saying the sentences. Pay attention to the /ɪŋ/ sound.

1 The animals are playing.
2 You're helping me.
3 Is she talking?
4 They're digging a hole.
5 She isn't getting up now.
6 They aren't walking.

Unit 5: /ɪ/ and /iː/

1 🔊 1.10 Listen to the words with the /ɪ/ and /iː/ sound.

/ɪ/	/iː/
crisps	sweets
sandwich	meat
milk	easy
fizzy drinks	cheese
chips	routine

2 Read the words. Which words have the sound /ɪ/ and which have the sound /iː/? Tick (✔) the correct column.

	/ɪ/	/iː/
drink		
fish		
meet		
people		
visit		
clean		
give		
pizza		
ice cream		

3 🔊 1.11 Listen and check your answers.

4 Add three more words to each group.

1 /ɪ/ sit, drink _____
2 /iː/ beans, eat _____

PRONUNCIATION BANK

Unit 6: Past tense -ed endings

1 🔊 1.12 **Listen to the past simple verbs and repeat.**

/d/   lived

/t/   liked

/ɪd/   started

2 🔊 1.13 **Listen to the verbs and pay attention to the -ed sound. Then complete the table.**

> ~~asked~~ invaded stayed changed invented visited checked practised wanted discovered preferred watched

/d/	/t/	/ɪd/
	asked	

3 🔊 1.14 **Listen and repeat the sentences.**

1 We stayed in Morocco last month.
2 She asked her teacher a question.
3 They visited New York last year.

4 **Choose a verb in each group with the /ɪd/ sound.**

1 played   hunted   finished   died
2 chased   danced   protected   worked
3 saved   shared   cooked   decided
4 chatted   walked   crossed   travelled

Unit 7: Diphthongs: /eɪ/, /aɪ/, /əʊ/ and /aʊ/

1 🔊 1.15 **Listen and repeat the words.**

/eɪ/	play	name	hate
/aɪ/	nice	like	buy
/əʊ/	go	poster	phone
/aʊ/	brown	how	about

2 **Choose a word in each group with the same sound as the words in bold.**

1 **now**   window   sound   short
2 **why**   find   crisp   win
3 **wait**   friend   snake   fair
4 **know**   clock   now   ago
5 **fly**   build   house   write
6 **town**   buy   owl   make

3 🔊 1.16 **Listen and check your answers.**

4 **Match the pairs of words with the same diphthong sound.**

1 stay   a eye
2 know   b late
3 ice   c note
4 mouse   d say
5 made   e out

Unit 8: Sentence stress and rhythm

1 🔊 1.17 **Listen and repeat. Pay attention to the stress on the important words.**

1 **Where** are you **going** to **stay**?
2 We're **going** to **stay** in a **tent**.

2 🔊 1.18 **Listen and repeat the sentences. Choose the stressed words in each sentence.**

1 Are you going to buy a torch?
2 Is he going to look for animals?
3 What are we going to see?
4 They're going to find some insects.
5 How is she going to travel?
6 I'm going to take some photos.

3 **Choose the unstressed words in each sentence.**

1 They're going to take some tents.
2 We're going to buy a map.
3 You're going to use the phone.
4 There's going to be a storm.
5 She's going to bring a stove.
6 It's going to snow.

4 **Practise saying the sentences from exercise 3.**

Phonetic symbols

Vowels

/i/	happy
/ɪ/	it
/iː/	he
/æ/	flag
/ɑː/	art
/e/	egg
/ɜː/	her
/ɒ/	not
/ɔː/	four
/ʊ/	look
/uː/	you
/ə/	sugar
/ʌ/	mum
/eɪ/	day
/aɪ/	why
/ɔɪ/	noisy
/aʊ/	how
/əʊ/	go
/ɪə/	here
/eə/	wear
/ʊə/	tourist

Consonants

/p/	pen
/b/	big
/t/	two
/d/	dog
/k/	can
/g/	good
/tʃ/	beach
/dʒ/	job
/f/	food
/v/	very
/θ/	think
/ð/	then
/s/	speak
/z/	zoo
/ʃ/	she
/ʒ/	television
/h/	house
/m/	meat
/n/	now
/ŋ/	sing
/l/	late
/r/	radio
/j/	yes
/w/	we

Starter unit

April (n)   /'eɪprəl/
August (n)   /'ɔːgəst/
bad (adj)   /bæd/
bag (n)   /bæg/
between (prep)   /bɪ'twiːn/
big (adj)   /bɪg/
board (n)   /bɔːd/
boring (adj)   /'bɔːrɪŋ/
boy (n)   /bɔɪ/
car (n)   /kɑː(r)/
CD player (n)   /siː 'diː ˌpleɪə(r)/
chair (n)   /tʃeə(r)/
cheap (adj)   /tʃiːp/
class (n)   /klɑːs/
classroom (n)   /'klɑːsruːm/
clock (n)   /klɒk/
December (n)   /dɪ'sembə(r)/
desk (n)   /desk/
dictionary (n)   /'dɪkʃənri/
difficult (adj)   /'dɪfɪkəlt/
door (n)   /dɔː(r)/
DVD (n)   /ˌdiː ˌviː 'diː/
easy (adj)   /'iːzi/
expensive (adj)   /ɪk'spensɪv/
February (n)   /'februəri/
Friday (n)   /'fraɪdeɪ/
good (adj)   /gʊd/
her (pron)   /hɜː(r)/
his (pron)   /hɪz/
horrible (adj)   /'hɒrəbl/
in (prep)   /ɪn/
interesting (adj)   /'ɪntrəstɪŋ/
its (pron)   /ɪts/
January (n)   /'dʒænjuəri/
June (n)   /dʒuːn/
July (n)   /dʒu'laɪ/
laptop (n)   /'læptɒp/
March (n)   /mɑːtʃ/
May (n)   /meɪ/
Monday (n)   /'mʌndeɪ/
my (pron)   /maɪ/
near (prep)   /nɪə(r)/
next to (prep)   /'neks ˌtuː, tə/
nice (adj)   /naɪs/
November (n)   /nəʊ'vembə(r)/
notebook (n)   /'nəʊtbʊk/
October (n)   /ɒk'təʊbə(r)/
on (prep)   /ɒn/
our (pron)   /'aʊə(r)/
pen (n)   /pen/
popular (adj)   /'pɒpjələ(r)/
poster (n)   /'pəʊstə(r)/
ruler (n)   /'ruːlə(r)/
Saturday (n)   /'sætədeɪ/
September (n)   /sep'tembə(r)/
shelf (n)   /ʃelf/
small (adj)   /smɔːl/
student (n)   /'stjuːdənt/
Sunday (n)   /'sʌndeɪ/
teacher (n)   /'tiːtʃə(r)/
their (pron)   /ðeə(r)/
Tuesday (n)   /'tjuːzdeɪ/
Thursday (n)   /'θɜːzdeɪ/
under (prep)   /'ʌndə(r)/
unpopular (adj)   /ʌn'pɒpjələ(r)/
Wednesday (n)   /'wenzdeɪ/
window (n)   /'wɪndəʊ/
your (pron)   /jɔː(r)/

Unit 1

about (prep)   /ə'baʊt/
actor (n)   /'æktə(r)/
and (conj)   /ænd, ənd/
animal (n)   /'ænɪml/
art (n)   /ɑːt/
artist (n)   /'ɑːtɪst/
basketball (n)   /'bɑːskɪtbɔːl/
birthday (n)   /'bɜːθdeɪ/
black (adj)   /blæk/
book (n)   /bʊk/
brother (n)   /'brʌðə(r)/
but (conj)   /bʌt, bət/
by (prep)   /baɪ/
camera (n)   /'kæmərə/
can't stand (v)   /ˌkɑːnt 'stænd/
CD (n)   /ˌsiː 'diː/
championship (n)   /'tʃæmpiənʃɪp/
chatting (on the internet)
    (n)   /'tʃætɪŋ (ˌɒn ðiː 'ɪntənet)/
classical (adj)   /'klæsɪkl/
colour (n)   /'kʌlə(r)/
computer (n)   /kəm'pjuːtə(r)/
computer game (n)   /kəm'pjuːtə
    ˌgeɪm/
cousin (n)   /'kʌzn/
cool (adj)   /kuːl/
critic (n)   /'krɪtɪk/
cycling (n)   /'saɪklɪŋ/
director (n)   /də'rektə(r),
    dɪ-, daɪ-/
dog (n)   /dɒg/
drummer (n)   /'drʌmə(r)/
email (n)   /'iːmeɪl/
English (n)   /'ɪŋglɪʃ/
especially (adv)   /ɪ'speʃəli/
expert (n)   /'ekspɜːt/
fan (n)   /fæn/
favourite (adj)   /'feɪvərɪt/
film (n)   /fɪlm/
football (n)   /'fʊtbɔːl/
friend (n)   /frend/
free time (n)   /ˌfriː 'taɪm/
from (prep)   /frɒm, frəm/
game (n)   /geɪm/
good at (adj)   /'gʊd ˌæt, ət/
green belt (n)   /'griːn ˌbelt/
group (n)   /gruːp/
guitar (n)   /gɪ'tɑː(r)/
hate (v)   /heɪt/

(Pop) group · bassist · drummer · guitarist · microphone · electric guitar · vocalist · bass guitar · drums · keyboard player · keyboards

have (v) /hæv/
have got (v) /ˌhæv ˈgɒt/
hip hop (n) /ˈhɪp ˌhɒp/
hobby (n) /ˈhɒbi/
how (pron) /haʊ/
how many (pron) /ˈhaʊ ˌmeni/
how old (pron) /haʊ ˌəʊld/
interested in (adj) /ˈɪntrəstɪd ˌɪn/
(I'm) into (adj) /ˈ(aɪm) ˌɪntə/
love (v) /lʌv/
mad about (adj) /ˈmæd əˌbaʊt/
martial arts (n) /ˌmɑːʃl ˈɑːts/
match (n) /mætʃ/
meeting friends (n) /ˌmiːtɪŋ ˈfrendz/
mouse (n) /maʊs/
music (n) /ˈmjuːzɪk/
name (n) /neɪm/
old (adj) /əʊld/
of (prep) /ɒv, əv/
or (conj) /ɔː(r)/
pet (n) /pet/
photo (n) /ˈfəʊtəʊ/
photography (n) /fəˈtɒgrəfi/
play (v) /pleɪ/
player (n) /ˈpleɪə(r)/
pop (n) /pɒp/
popular (adj) /ˈpɒpjələ(r)/
poster (n) /ˈpəʊstə(r)/
prefer (v) /prɪˈfɜː(r)/
programme (n) /ˈprəʊgræm/
rat (n) /ræt/
really (adv) /ˈriːəli/

science fiction (n) /ˈsaɪəns ˈfɪkʃn/
see (v) /siː/
singer (n) /ˈsɪŋə(r)/
skateboarding (n) /ˈskeɪtbɔːdɪŋ/
skiing (n) /ˈskiːɪŋ/
sport (n) /spɔːt/
surfing (n) /ˈsɜːfɪŋ/
swimming (n) /ˈswɪmɪŋ/
taekwondo (n) /taɪˈkwɒndəʊ/
team (n) /tiːm/
tennis (n) /ˈtenɪs/
that (det) /ðæt/
these (det) /ðiːz/
thing (n) /θɪŋ/
this (det) /ðɪs/
those (pron) /ðəʊz/
TV programme (n) /ˌtiː ˈviː ˌprəʊgræm/
watching TV (n) /ˌwɒtʃɪŋ ˌtiː ˈviː/
webcam (n) /ˈwebkæm/
website (n) /ˈwebsaɪt/
what (pron) /wɒt/
when (pron) /wen/
where (pron) /weə(r)/
who (pron) /huː/
writer (n) /ˈraɪtə(r)/

Unit 2

a (article) /ə/
amazing (adj) /əˈmeɪzɪŋ/
an (article) /ən/
any (det) /ˈeni/

art gallery (n) /ˈɑːt ˌgæləri/
article (n) /ˈɑːtɪkl/
building (n) /ˈbɪldɪŋ/
bus (n) /bʌs/
bus station (n) /ˈbʌs ˌsteɪʃn/
café (n) /ˈkæfeɪ/
car park (n) /ˈkɑː ˌpɑːk/
cinema (n) /ˈsɪnəmə/
city (n) /ˈsɪti/
city centre (n) /ˌsɪti ˈsentə(r)/
clean (adj) /kliːn/
coach (n) /kəʊtʃ/
dangerous (adj) /ˈdeɪndʒərəs/
desert (n) /ˈdezət/
dirty (adj) /ˈdɜːti/
enormous (adj) /ɪˈnɔːməs/
exciting (adj) /ɪkˈsaɪtɪŋ/
factory (n) /ˈfæktəri/
fantastic (adj) /fænˈtæstɪk/
fast (adj) /fɑːst/
flats (noun pl) /flæts/
floor (n) /flɔː(r)/
friendly (adj) /ˈfrendli/
glass (n) /glɑːs/
gym (n) /dʒɪm/
hospital (n) /ˈhɒspɪtl/
hotel (n) /həʊˈtel/
incredible (adj) /ɪnˈkredəbl/
lake (n) /leɪk/
large (adj) /lɑːdʒ/
library (n) /ˈlaɪbrəri/
lift (n) /lɪft/
luxury (adj) /ˈlʌkʃəri/
modern (adj) /ˈmɒdn/

noisy (adj)   /ˈnɔɪzi/
office (n)   /ˈɒfɪs/
on (prep)   /ɒn/
old (adj)   /əʊld/
park (n)   /pɑːk/
plane (n)   /pleɪn/
pretty (adj)   /ˈprɪti/
quiet (adj)   /ˈkwaɪət/
restaurant (n)   /ˈrestrɒnt/
river (n)   /ˈrɪvə(r)/
safe (adj)   /seɪf/
school (n)   /skuːl/
shopping centre (n)   /ˈʃɒpɪŋ ˌsentə(r)/
shop (n)   /ʃɒp/
skyscraper (n)   /ˈskaɪskreɪpə(r)/
some (det)   /sʌm, səm/
sports centre (n)   /ˈspɔːts ˌsentə(r)/
stairs (n)   /steəz/
supermarket (n)   /ˈsuːpəmɑːkɪt/
temperature (n)   /ˈtemprətʃə(r)/
there is (adv)   /ˌðeər ˈɪz/
there are (adv)   /ˌðeər ˈɑː(r)/
tiny (adj)   /ˈtaɪni/
tourism (n)   /ˈtʊərɪzəm/
tower (n)   /ˈtaʊə(r)/
town (n)   /taʊn/
train (n)   /treɪn/
train station (n)   /ˈtreɪn ˌsteɪʃn/
transport (n)   /ˈtrænspɔːt/
ugly (adj)   /ˈʌgli/
unfriendly (adj)   /ʌnˈfrendli/

Unit 3

always (adv)   /ˈɔːlweɪz/
America (n)   /əˈmerɪkə/
American (adj)   /əˈmerɪkən/
Australia (n)   /ɒˈstreɪliə/
Australian (adj)   /ɒˈstreɪliən/
border (n)   /ˈbɔːdə(r)/
Brazil (n)   /brəˈzɪl/
Brazilian (adj)   /brəˈzɪliən/
British (adj)   /ˈbrɪtɪʃ/
buy (v)   /baɪ/
Canada (n)   /ˈkænədə/
Canadian (adj)   /kəˈneɪdiən/
capital (city) (n)   /ˈkæpɪtl (ˌsɪti)/
capital letter (n)   /ˌkæpɪtl ˈletə/
China (n)   /ˈtʃaɪnə/
Chinese (adj)   /tʃaɪˈniːz/
class (n)   /ˈklɑːs/
come (v)   /kʌm/
comma (n)   /ˈkɒmə/
country (n)   /ˈkʌntri/
culture (n)   /ˈkʌltʃə(r)/
currency (n)   /ˈkʌrənsi/
daily routine (n)   /ˌdeɪli ruːˈtiːn/
dinner (n)   /ˈdɪnə(r)/
do (v)   /duː/
eat (v)   /iːt/
evening (n)   /ˈiːvnɪŋ/

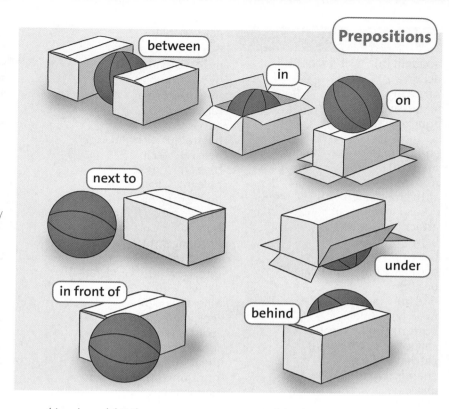

Prepositions

between
in
on
next to
under
in front of
behind

every (day / year) (det)
   /ˌevri ˈ(deɪ, jɪə)/
family (n)   /ˈfæməli/
finish (v)   /ˈfɪnɪʃ/
food (n)   /fuːd/
football (n)   /ˈfʊtbɔːl/
France (n)   /frɑːns/
French (adj)   /frentʃ/
fluently (adv)   /ˈfluːəntli/
German (adj)   /ˈdʒɜːmən/
Germany (n)   /ˈdʒɜːməni/
get up (v)   /ˌget ˈʌp/
go (v)   /gəʊ/
go to bed (v)   /ˌgəʊ tə ˈbed/
go to school (v)   /ˌgəʊ tə ˈskuːl/
have (lunch) (v)   /ˌhæv ˈlʌntʃ/
hello (exp)   /həˈləʊ/
Italian (n)   /ɪˈtæliən/
Italy (n)   /ˈɪtəli/
Japan (n)   /dʒəˈpæn/
Japanese (adj)   /dʒæpəˈniːz/
know (v)   /nəʊ/
language (n)   /ˈlæŋgwɪdʒ/
like (v)   /laɪk/
live (v)   /lɪv/
make (v)   /meɪk/
Mandarin (n)   /ˈmændərɪn/
mix (v)   /mɪks/
morning (n)   /ˈmɔːnɪŋ/
nationality (n)   /næʃəˈnæləti/
never (adv)   /ˈnevə(r)/
o'clock (adv)   /əˈklɒk/
often (adv)   /ˈɒfn, ˈɒftən/
parent (n)   /ˈpeərənt/
people (noun pl)   /ˈpiːpl/

person (n)   /ˈpɜːsn/
play (v)   /pleɪ/
Poland (n)   /ˈpəʊlənd/
Polish (adj)   /ˈpəʊlɪʃ/
population (n)   /pɒpjuˈleɪʃn/
read (v)   /riːd/
religion (n)   /rɪˈlɪdʒən/
school (n)   /ˌskuːl/
shop (n)   /ʃɒp/
sleep (v)   /sliːp/
sometimes (adv)   /ˈsʌmtaɪmz/
South America (n)   /ˌsaʊθ əˈmerɪkə/
Spain (n)   /speɪn/
Spanish (adj)   /ˈspænɪʃ/
speak (v)   /spiːk/
start (v)   /stɑːt/
student (n)   /ˈstjuːdnt/
study (v)   /ˈstʌdi/
teach (v)   /tiːtʃ/
teacher (n)   /ˈtiːtʃə(r)/
trumpet (n)   /ˈtrʌmpɪt/
try (v)   /traɪ/
the UK (n)   /ðə ˌjuː ˈkeɪ/
the USA (n)   /ðə ˌjuː ˌes ˈeɪ/
understand (v)   /ʌndəˈstænd/
use (v)   /juːz/
usually (adv)   /ˈjuːʒuəli/
watch (v)   /wɒtʃ/
watch (TV) (v)   /wɒtʃ ˌtiː ˈviː/
weekend (n)   /wiːkˈend/
word (n)   /wɜːd/
work (n)   /wɜːk/
write (v)   /raɪt/

Unit 4

accident (n)   /'æksɪdənt/
action (n)   /'ækʃn/
Africa (n)   /'æfrɪkə/
aggressive (adj)   /ə'gresɪv/
approximately (adv)
  /ə'prɒksɪmətli/
aquarium (n)   /ə'kweəriəm/
Arctic (n)   /'ɑːktɪk/
Asia (n)   /'eɪʒə/
at the moment (prep)   /ət ðə
  'məʊmənt/
attack (v)   /ə'tæk/
baby (n)   /'beɪbi/
bear (n)   /beə(r)/
because (conj)   /bɪ'kɒz, bɪ'kəz/
bee (n)   /biː/
bird (n)   /bɜːd/
build (v)   /bɪld/
butterfly (n)   /'bʌtəflaɪ/
calf (of killer whale) (n)   /kɑːf/
catch (v)   /kætʃ/
chameleon (n)   /kə'miːliən/
chase (v)   /tʃeɪs/
chick (n)   /tʃɪk/
climate (n)   /'klaɪmət/
climb (v)   /klaɪm/
crocodile (n)   /'krɒkədaɪl/
cub (of polar bear) (n)   /kʌb/
die (v)   /daɪ/
dig (v)   /dɪg/
dolphin (n)   /'dɒlfɪn/
eat (v)   /iːt/
elephant (n)   /'elɪfənt/
endangered (adj)   /ɪn'deɪndʒəd/
(become) extinct (adj)   /(bɪ,kʌm)
  ɪk'stɪŋkt/
falcon (n)   /'fɔːlkən/
feed (v)   /fiːd/

fight (v)   /faɪt/
fish (n)   /fɪʃ/
fly (n)   /flaɪ/
fly (v)   /flaɪ/
frog (n)   /frɒg/
fur (n)   /fɜː(r)/
grass (n)   /grɑːs/
habitat (n)   /'hæbɪtæt/
help (v)   /help/
hide (v)   /'haɪd/
hole (n)   /həʊl/
house (n)   /haʊs/
human (n)   /'hjuːmən/
hunt (v)   /hʌnt/
(in) danger (n)   /ˌɪn 'deɪndʒə(r)/
insect (n)   /'ɪnsekt/
interview (n)   /ˌɪntəvjuː/
kill (v)   /kɪl/
killer whale (n)   /'kɪlə ˌweɪl/
look at (v)   /'lʊk ˌæt, ət/
look for (v)   /'lʊk ˌfɔː(r), fə(r)/
look like (v)   /'lʊk ˌlaɪk/
meat (n)   /miːt/
mosquito (n)   /mə'skiːtəʊ/
nation (n)   /'neɪʃn/
nature (n)   /'neɪtʃə(r)/
newspaper (n)   /'njuːspeɪpə(r)/
orca (n)   /'ɔːkə/
owl (n)   /aʊl/
parrot (n)   /'pærət/
play (with) (v)   /'pleɪ ˌ(wɪð)/
polar bear (n)   /ˌpəʊlə 'beə(r)/
pollution (n)   /pə'luːʃn/
protect (v)   /prə'tekt/
rabbit (n)   /'ræbɪt/
read (v)   /riːd/
rock (n)   /rɒk/
run (v)   /rʌn/
salmon (n)   /'sæmən/
save (v)   /seɪv/

sea (n)   /siː/
seal (n)   /siːl/
sing (v)   /sɪŋ/
shark (n)   /ʃɑːk/
shore (n)   /ʃɔː(r)/
snake (n)   /sneɪk/
spider (n)   /'spaɪdə(r)/
sleep (v)   /sliːp/
sounds like (v)   /'saʊndz ˌlaɪk/
squid (n)   /skwɪd/
swim (v)   /swɪm/
tiger (n)   /'taɪgə(r)/
tree (n)   /triː/
turtle (n)   /'tɜːtl/
use (v)   /juːz/
wasp (n)   /wɒsp/
whale (n)   /weɪl/
zoo (n)   /zuː/

Unit 5

a lot of (det)   /ə 'lɒt əv/
abroad (adv)   /ə'brɔːd/
aluminium (n)   /ˌæljə'mɪniəm/
any (det)   /'eni/
apple (n)   /'æpl/
art (n)   /ɑːt/
basketball (n)   /'bɑːskɪtbɔːl/
busy (adj)   /'bɪzi/
beans (noun pl)   /biːnz/
Belgium (n)   /'beldʒəm/
boarding school (n)   /'bɔːdɪŋ ˌskuːl/
bread (n)   /bred/
burger (n)   /'bɜːgə/
cafeteria (n)   /ˌkæfə'tɪəriə/
canteen (n)   /kæn'tiːn/
chat (with friends) (v)   /ˌtʃæt wɪð
  'frendz/
cheese (n)   /tʃiːz/
chess (n)   /tʃes/

Geographical features

mountain

waterfall

hill

valley

lake

forest

river

beach

ocean

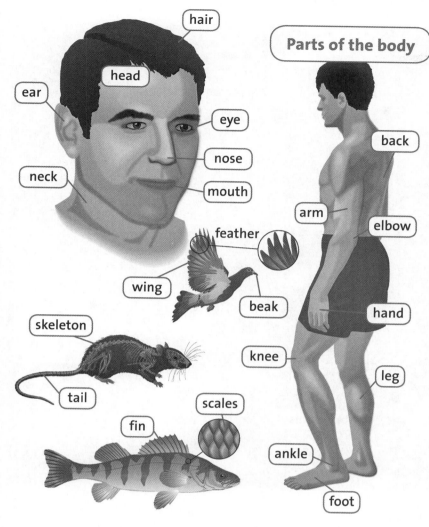

Parts of the body

- hair
- head
- ear
- eye
- nose
- neck
- mouth
- back
- arm
- elbow
- feather
- wing
- beak
- hand
- skeleton
- knee
- leg
- tail
- scales
- fin
- ankle
- foot

chicken (n)   /ˈtʃɪkɪn/
chips (noun pl)   /tʃɪps/
chocolate (n)   /ˈtʃɒklət/
crisps (noun pl)   /krɪsps/
dance (v)   /dɑːns/
dish (n)   /dɪʃ/
drama (n)   /ˈdrɑːmə/
drink (v)   /drɪŋk/
eat (v)   /iːt/
egg (n)   /eg/
exam (n)   /ɪgˈzæm/
fish (n)   /fɪʃ/
fizzy drink (n)   /ˌfɪzi ˈdrɪŋk/
food (n)   /fuːd/
football (n)   /ˈfʊtbɔːl/
French (n)   /frentʃ/
fruit (n)   /fruːt/
geography (n)   /dʒiˈɒgrəfi/
gigabyte (n)   /ˈgɪgəbaɪt/
grapes (noun pl)   /greɪps/
handball (n)   /ˈhændbɔːl/
(have) a break (n)   /ˌ(hæv) ə ˈbreɪk/
history (n)   /ˈhɪstri/
homework (n)   /ˈhəʊmwɜːk/
homesick (adj)   /ˈhəʊmsɪk/
ice cream (n)   /ˌaɪs ˈkriːm/
ICT (n)   /ˌaɪ ˌsiː ˈtiː/

jeans (n)   /dʒiːnz/
(orange) juice (n)   /ˈ(ɒrɪndʒ) ˌdʒuːs/
junk food (n)   /ˈdʒʌŋk ˌfuːd/
magnesium (n)   /mægˈniːziəm/
many (det)   /ˈmeni/
match (n)   /mætʃ/
maths (n)   /mæθs/
meat (n)   /miːt/
megabyte (n)   /ˈmegəbaɪt/
much (det)   /mʌtʃ/
neon (n)   /ˈniːɒn/
nuts (noun pl)   /nʌts/
oxygen (n)   /ˈɒksɪdʒən/
orchestra (n)   /ˈɔːkɪstrə/
pasta (n)   /ˈpæstə/
PE (n)   /ˌpiː ˈiː/
pear (n)   /peə(r)/
pizza (n)   /ˈpiːtsə/
potato (n)   /pəˈteɪtəʊ/
practice (n)   /ˈpræktɪs/
practise (v)   /ˈpræktɪs/
rice (n)   /raɪs/
rugby (n)   /ˈrʌgbi/
rule (n)   /ruːl/
salad (n)   /ˈsæləd/
sandwich (n)   /ˈsænwɪtʃ/
science (n)   /ˈsaɪəns/

self-service (adj)   /ˌself ˈsɜːvɪs/
sit (v)   /sɪt/
share (a room) (v)   /ˌʃeər
   (ə ˈruːm)/
snack (n)   /snæk/
some (det)   /sʌm, səm/
soup (n)   /suːp/
stand (v)   /stænd/
subject (n)   /ˈsʌbdʒɪkt/
sweets (noun pl)   /swiːts/
swimming pool (n)   /ˈswɪmɪŋ ˌpuːl/
table tennis (n)   /ˈteɪbl ˌtenɪs/
tango (n)   /ˈtæŋgəʊ/
terabyte (n)   /ˈterəbaɪt/
test (n)   /test/
vegetables (noun pl)   /ˈvedʒtəblz/
vegetarian (adj)   /vedʒəˈteəriən/
vending machine (n)
   /ˈvendɪŋ məˌʃiːn/
water (n)   /ˈwɔːtə(r)/
work (v)   /wɜːk/
work (abroad) (v)   /ˌwɜːk (əˈbrɔːd)/

Unit 6

actor (n)   /ˈæktə(r)/
artist (n)   /ˈɑːtɪst/
astronaut (n)   /ˈæstrənɔːt/
Atlantic Ocean (n)   /ətˌlæntɪk
   ˈəʊʃn/
arrive (v)   /əˈraɪv/
Bahamas (n)   /bəˈhɑːməz/
brand name (n)   /ˈbrænd ˌneɪm/
builder (n)   /ˈbɪldə(r)/
businessman/woman (n)
   /ˈbɪznəsmæn, wʊmən/
call (v)   /kɔːl/
celebrity (n)   /səˈlebrəti/
change (v)   /tʃeɪndʒ/
chef (n)   /ʃef/
common (adj)   /ˈkɒmən/
cross (v)   /krɒs/
cut (v)   /kʌt/
discover (v)   /dɪˈskʌvə(r)/
doctor (n)   /ˈdɒktə(r)/
Egypt (n)   /ˈiːdʒɪpt/
element (n)   /ˈelɪmənt/
explore (v)   /ɪkˈsplɔː(r)/
explorer (n)   /ɪkˈsplɔːrə(r)/
farmer (n)   /ˈfɑːmə(r)/
fire (n)   /ˈfaɪə(r)/
firefighter (n)   /ˈfaɪə ˌfaɪtə(r)/
first name (n)   /ˈfɜːst ˌneɪm/
garage (n)   /ˈgærɑːʒ/
hairdresser (n)   /ˈheədresə(r)/
hard (adj)   /hɑːd/
horse (n)   /hɔːs/
insect (n)   /ˈɪnsekt/
invade (v)   /ɪnˈveɪd/
invent (v)   /ɪnˈvent/
inventor (n)   /ɪnˈventə(r)/

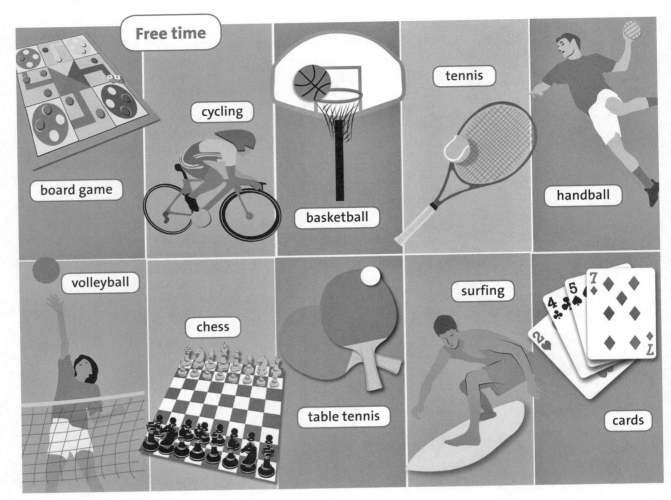

Free time

board game · cycling · basketball · tennis · handball · volleyball · chess · table tennis · surfing · cards

island (n)   /ˈaɪlənd/
job (n)   /dʒɒb/
king (n)   /kɪŋ/
make (v)   /meɪk/
mechanic (n)   /məˈkænɪk/
middle name (n)   /ˈmɪdl ˌneɪm/
musician (n)   /mjuːˈzɪʃn/
Native Indian (n)   /ˌneɪtɪv ˈɪndɪən/
nickname (n)   /ˈnɪkneɪm/
Nobel prize (n)   /ˈnəʊbel ˌpraɪz/
nurse (n)   /nɜːs/
place (n)   /pleɪs/
plane (n)   /pleɪn/
port (n)   /pɔːt/
queen (n)   /kwiːn/
radioactive (adj)   /reɪdiəʊˈæktɪv/
radium (n)   /ˈreɪdiəm/
Romans (noun pl)   /ˈrəʊmənz/
scientist (n)   /ˈsaɪəntɪst/
ship (n)   /ʃɪp/
stay (v)   /steɪ/
stop (v)   /stɒp/
surname (n)   /ˈsɜːneɪm/
teacher (n)   /ˈtiːtʃə(r)/
telephone (n)   /ˈtelɪfəʊn/
today (n)   /təˈdeɪ/
travel (v)   /ˈtrævl/
village (n)   /ˈvɪlɪdʒ/

visit (v)   /ˈvɪzɪt/
waiter (n)   /ˈweɪtə(r)/
waitress (n)   /ˈweɪtrəs/
wash (v)   /wɒʃ/
well-paid (adj)   /ˌwel ˈpeɪd/
writer (n)   /ˈraɪtə(r)/
yesterday (n)   /ˈjestədeɪ/

Unit 7

arcade (games) (n)   /ɑːˈkeɪd
   (ˌgeɪmz)/
avatar (n)   /ˈævətɑː(r)/
average (height / build) (det)
   /ˈævərɪdʒ/
barbecue (n)   /ˈbɑːbɪkjuː/
beard (n)   /bɪəd/
beat (someone) (v)   /ˈbiːt …/
blonde (adj)   /blɒnd/
blue (adj)   /bluː/
break (a record) (v)   /ˌbreɪk
   (ə ˈrekɔːd)/
brown (adj)   /braʊn/
champion (n)   /ˈtʃæmpiən/
choose (v)   /tʃuːz/
choice (n)   /tʃɔɪs/
competition (n)   /kɒmpəˈtɪʃn/
console (n)   /ˈkɒnsəʊl/

create (v)   /kriˈeɪt/
creator (n)   /kriˈeɪtə(r)/
curly (adj)   /ˈkɜːli/
creative (adj)   /kriˈeɪtɪv/
dark (adj)   /dɑːk/
design (v)   /dɪˈzaɪn/
designer (n)   /dɪˈzaɪnə(r)/
detective (n)   /dɪˈtektɪv/
entertain (v)   /entəˈteɪn/
entertainment (n)   /entəˈteɪnmənt/
fair (adj)   /feə(r)/
famous (adj)   /ˈfeɪməs/
fat (adj)   /fæt/
game (n)   /geɪm/
glasses (n)   /ˈglɑːsɪz/
great (adj)   /greɪt/
green (adj)   /griːn/
hair (n)   /heə(r)/
hair colour (n)   /ˈheə ˌkʌlə(r)/
holiday (n)   /ˈhɒlədeɪ/
ice-hockey (n)   /ˈaɪs ˌhɒki/
imagine (v)   /ɪˈmædʒɪn/
imagination (n)   /ɪˌmædʒɪˈneɪʃn/
long (adj)   /lɒŋ/
lose (a game) (v)   /ˌluːz ə ˈgeɪm/
medal (n)   /ˈmedl/
memory (n)   /ˈmeməri/
motor racing (n)   /ˈməʊtə ˌreɪsɪŋ/
moustache (n)   /məˈstɑːʃ/

Jobs

scientist

receptionist

businessman

reporter

referee

shop assistant

waiter

lawyer

museum (n) /mjuˈziːəm/
overweight (adj) /ˌəʊvəˈweɪt/
party (n) /ˈpɑːti/
play (a game) (v) /ˌpleɪ (ə ˈgeɪm)/
player (n) /ˈpleɪə/
poison (n) /ˈpɔɪzn/
positive (adj) /ˈpɒzətɪv/
quite (short) (det) /ˌkwaɪt ˈ(ʃɔːt)/
race (n) /reɪs/
remember (v) /rɪˈmembə(r)/
run (a race) (v) /ˌrʌn ə ˈreɪs/
score (a goal) (v) /ˌskɔːr ə ˈgəʊl/
short (adj) /ʃɔːt/
slim (adj) /slɪm/
straight (adj) /streɪt/
take part (in a competition) (v)
    /ˌteɪk ˌpɑːt (ɪn ə kɒmpəˈtɪʃn)/
tall (adj) /tɔːl/
theme park (n) /ˈθiːm ˌpɑːk/
think (v) /θɪŋk/
toy (n) /tɔɪ/
trophy (n) /ˈtrəʊfi/
video game (n) /ˈvɪdiəʊ ˌgeɪm/
violent (adj) /ˈvaɪələnt/
volleyball (n) /ˈvɒlibɔːl/
win (a race) (v) /ˌwɪn ə ˈreɪs/
world record (n) /ˌwɜːld ˈrekɔːd/

Unit 8

angry (adj) /ˈæŋgri/
attack (v) /əˈtæk/
bring (v) /brɪŋ/
camp (n) /ˈkæmp/
camping (n) /ˈkæmpɪŋ/

campsite (n) /ˈkæmpsaɪt/
carry (v) /ˈkæri/
caving (n) /ˈkeɪvɪŋ/
cloud (n) /klaʊd/
cloudy (adj) /ˈklaʊdi/
cold (adj) /kəʊld/
compass (n) /ˈkʌmpəs/
excited (adj) /ɪkˈsaɪtɪd/
expedition (n) /ekspəˈdɪʃn/
explore (v) /ɪkˈsplɔː(r)/
first-aid kit (n) /ˌfɜːst ˈeɪd ˌkɪt/
fog (n) /fɒg/
foggy (adj) /ˈfɒgi/
forget (v) /fəˈget/
gloves (n) /glʌvz/
gorilla (n) /gəˈrɪlə/
heat (n) /hiːt/
helmet (n) /ˈhelmɪt/
hot (adj) /hɒt/
ice (n) /aɪs/
icy (adj) /ˈaɪsi/
insect repellent (n) /ˈɪnsekt rɪˌpelənt/
jeep (n) /dʒiːp/
jungle (n) /ˈdʒʌŋgl/
kayak (n) /ˈkaɪæk/
kayaking (n) /ˈkaɪækɪŋ/
look (v) /lʊk/
map (n) /mæp/
miserable (adj) /ˈmɪzrəbl/
monkey (n) /ˈmʌŋki/
mountain (n) /ˈmaʊntən/
mountain biking (n) /ˈmaʊntən
    ˌbaɪkɪŋ/
paragliding (n) /ˈpærəglaɪdɪŋ/
phone (n) /fəʊn/

rain (n) /reɪn/
rainy (adj) /ˈreɪni/
remember (v) /rɪˈmembə(r)/
rock climbing (n) /ˈrɒk ˌklaɪmɪŋ/
rope (n) /rəʊp/
rucksack (n) /ˈrʌksæk/
satellite (n) /ˈsætəlaɪt/
scared (adj) /skeəd/
sleeping bag (n) /ˈsliːpɪŋ ˌbæg/
snow (n) /snəʊ/
snowboarding (n) /ˈsnəʊbɔːdɪŋ/
snowy (adj) /ˈsnəʊi/
storm (n) /stɔːm/
stormy (adj) /ˈstɔːmi/
stove (n) /stəʊv/
sun (n) /sʌn/
sunny (adj) /ˈsʌni/
sunglasses (n) /ˈsʌnglɑːsɪz/
sunscreen (n) /ˈsʌnskriːn/
survival (n) /səˈvaɪvl/
survive (v) /səˈvaɪv/
swim (v) /swɪm/
take (v) /teɪk/
tent (n) /tent/
torch (n) /tɔːtʃ/
trekking (n) /ˈtrekɪŋ/
use (v) /juːz/
warm (clothes) (adj) /ˌwɔːm
    (ˈkləʊðz)/
waterproof clothes (noun pl)
    /ˌwɔːtəpruːf ˈkləʊðz/
wear (v) /weə(r)/
weather (n) /ˈweðə/
wind (n) /wɪnd/
windy (adj) /ˈwɪndi/

Times

 five past three

 ten past three

 quarter past three

 twenty past three

 twenty-five past three

 half past three

 twenty-five to four

 twenty to four

 quarter to four

 ten to four

 five to four

 midday/midnight

worried (adj) /ˈwʌrid/

English Plus Options

Extra listening and speaking

Unit 1
at the back (prep) /ət ðə ˈbæk/
in the middle (prep) /ˌɪn ðə ˈmɪdl/
on the left (prep) /ˌɒn ðə ˈleft/
on the right (prep) /ˌɒn ðə ˈraɪt/
next to (prep) /ˈnekst ˌtuː, tə/

Unit 2
at (prep) /æt, ət/
dot (n) /dɒt/
double (six) (adj) /ˌdʌbl ˈ(sɪks)/
email address (n) /ˈiːmeɪl əˌdres/
phone number (n) /ˈfəʊn ˌnʌmbə(r)/
postcode (n) /ˈpəʊstkəʊd/
zero (n) /ˈzɪərəʊ/

Unit 3
timetable (n) /ˈtaɪmteɪbl/
what time (pron) /ˈwɒt ˌtaɪm/

Unit 4
date (n) /deɪt/
first (n) /fɜːst/
second (n) /ˈsekənd/
third (n) /θɜːd/

Unit 5
how much (pron) /ˈhaʊ ˌmʌtʃ/
pence (n) /pens/
pound (currency) (n) /paʊnd/

Unit 6
adventure (n) /ədˈventʃə(r)/
comedy (n) /ˈkɒmədi/
fantasy (n) /ˈfæntəsi/
horror (n) /ˈhɒrə(r)/
love (n) /lʌv/

Unit 7
action (n) /ˈækʃn/
driving (n) /ˈdraɪvɪŋ/
racing (n) /ˈreɪsɪŋ/
simulation (n) /sɪmjuˈleɪʃn/

Unit 8
cloud (n) /klaʊd/
degrees (n) /dɪˈɡriːz/
east (n) /iːst/
north (n) /nɔːθ/
rain (n, v) /reɪn/
south (n) /saʊθ/
sun (n) /ˈsʌn/
weather forecast (n) /ˈweðə ˌfɔːkɑːst/
west (n) /west/

Curriculum Extra

Unit 1
blue (adj) /bluː/
complementary (adj) /kɒmplɪˈmentri/
contrast (n) /ˈkɒntrɑːst/
cool (adj) /ˈkuːl/
green (adj) /ɡriːn/
orange (adj) /ˈɒrɪndʒ/
primary (colour) (adj) /ˈpraɪməri ˌkʌlə/
purple (adj) /ˈpɜːpl/
red (adj) /red/

secondary (adj) /ˈsekəndri/
warm (adj) /wɔːm/
yellow (adj) /ˈjeləʊ/

Unit 2
area (n) /ˈeəriə/
circle (n) /ˈsɜːkl/
forest (n) /ˈfɒrɪst/
hill (n) /hɪl/
kilometre (n) /ˈkɪləmiːtə(r)/
legend (n) /ˈledʒənd/
(X metres) high (adj) /(ˌ... ˌmiːtəz) ˈhaɪ/
path (n) /pɑːθ/
railway (n) /ˈreɪlweɪ/
representation (n) /ˌreprɪzenˈteɪʃn/
river (n) /ˈrɪvə(r)/
road (n) /rəʊd/
scale (n) /skeɪl/
triangle (n) /ˈtraɪæŋɡl/

Unit 3
angry (adj) /ˈæŋɡri/
communicate (v) /kəˈmjuːnɪkeɪt/
confused (adj) /kənˈfjuːzd/
facial expression (n) /ˌfeɪʃl ɪkˈspreʃn/
gesture (n) /ˈdʒestʃə(r)/
happy (adj) /ˈhæpi/
Mandarin (n) /ˈmændərɪn/
surprised (adj) /səˈpraɪzd/
tired (adj) /ˈtaɪəd/
non-verbal (adj) /ˌnɒnˈvɜːbl/
verbal (adj) /ˈvɜːbl/

Unit 4
amphibian (n) /æmˈfɪbiən/

Describing people

 happy

 tired

 confused

angry

 surprised

 sad

 bored

 frightened

 embarrassed

backbone (n)   /ˈbækbəʊn/
bird (n)   /bɜːd/
feather (n)   /ˈfeðə(r)/
female (n)   /ˈfiːmeɪl/
fin (n)   /fɪn/
fish (n)   /fɪʃ/
fishing net (n)   /ˈfɪʃɪŋ ˌnet/
gills (noun pl)   /ɡɪlz/
hair (n)   /heə(r)/
kiwi (n)   /ˈkiːwiː/
legs (noun pl)   /leɡz/
lizard (n)   /ˈlɪzəd/
lungs (noun pl)   /lʌŋz/
mammal (n)   /ˈmæml/
natural science (n)   /ˌnætʃrəl ˈsaɪəns/
on land (prep)   /ˌɒn ˈlænd/
ostrich (n)   /ˈɒstrɪtʃ/
reptile (n)   /ˈreptaɪl/
scales (noun pl)   /skeɪlz/
vertebrate (n)   /ˈvɜːtɪbrət/
wings (noun pl)   /wɪŋz/

Unit 5
aim (v)   /eɪm/
basket (n)   /ˈbɑːskɪt/
bounce (v)   /baʊns/
catch (v)   /kætʃ/
court (n)   /kɔːt/
kick (v)   /kɪk/
pass (v)   /pɑːs/
score (v)   /skɔː(r)/
shoot (v)   /ʃuːt/
substitute (n)   /ˈsʌbstɪtjuːt/
throw (v)   /θrəʊ/

Unit 6
character (n)   /ˈkærəktə(r)/
god (n)   /ɡɒd/
goddess (n)   /ˈɡɒdes/
Norse (adj)   /nɔːs/
strong (adj)   /strɒŋ/
thunder (n)   /ˈθʌndə(r)/

war (n)   /wɔː(r)/

Unit 7
download (v)   /daʊnˈləʊd/
internet (n)   /ˈɪntənet/
information (n)   /ɪnfəˈmeɪʃn/
invention (n)   /ɪnˈvenʃn/
symbol (n)   /ˈsɪmbl/
technology (n)   /tekˈnɒlədʒi/

Unit 8
(the) air (n)   /(ðiː) ˈeə(r)/
condensation (n)   /ˌkɒndenˈseɪʃn/
evaporation (n)   /ɪˌvæpəˈreɪʃn/
ocean (n)   /ˈəʊʃn/
precipitation (n)   /prɪˌsɪpɪˈteɪʃn/
transpiration (n)   /ˌtrænspɪˈreɪʃn/
water cycle (n)   /ˈwɔːtə ˌsaɪkl/
water vapour (n)   /ˈwɔːtə ˌveɪpə(r)/

Culture

Unit 1
around (the world) (prep)   /əˌraʊnd (ðə ˈwɜːld)/
team (n)   /tiːm/

Unit 2
historic (adj)   /hɪˈstɒrɪk/
tour (n)   /tʊə(r)/
university (n)   /juːnɪˈvɜːsəti/

Unit 3
chat room (n)   /ˈtʃæt ˌruːm/
official (adj)   /əˈfɪʃl/

Unit 4
attraction (n)   /əˈtrækʃn/
elk (n)   /elk/
rare (adj)   /reə(r)/
wild (adj)   /waɪld/
wolf (n)   /wʊlf/

wolves (noun pl)   /wʊlvz/

Unit 5
home-educated (adj)   /ˌhəʊm ˈedʒukeɪtɪd/
home schooling (n)   /ˌhəʊm ˈskuːlɪŋ/
lonely (adj)   /ˈləʊnli/

Unit 6
bath (n)   /bɑːθ/
Britannia (n)   /brɪˈtæniə/
invasion (n)   /ɪnˈveɪʒn/
public bath (n)   /ˌpʌblɪk ˈbɑːθ/
uniform (n)   /ˈjuːnɪfɔːm/

Unit 7
board game (n)   /ˈbɔːd ˌɡeɪm/
card game (n)   /ˈkɑːd ˌɡeɪm/
land on (a square) (v)   /ˌlænd ˌɒn ə ˈskweə/
member (of family) (n)   /ˈmembə(r)/
snakes and ladders (n)   /ˌsneɪks ən ˈlædəz/
strategy (n)   /ˈstrætədʒi/
traditional (adj)   /trəˈdɪʃənl/

Unit 8
climber (n)   /ˈklaɪmə(r)/
expedition (n)   /ekspəˈdɪʃn/
oxygen (n)   /ˈɒksɪdʒən/
sporty (adj)   /ˈspɔːti/
summit (n)   /ˈsʌmɪt/

Starter unit

Checking meaning and spelling and where things are

How do you say 'fenêtre' in English?
Sorry, can you say that again?
How do you spell that?
What's this in English?
Where's your dictionary?
It's on the shelf.

Emphasizing things

It's a **really** boring DVD.
She's a **very** nice teacher.
This book **isn't very** difficult.

Unit 1

How to talk about interests

I really like …. I like …. I don't like …. I love ….
I really hate …. I'm into …. I'm not into ….
  I'm interested in …. I'm not interested in ….

Greeting and meeting people

How are things?
This is (Tina).
Good to you meet you.
Are you into (surfing)?
What part of (the USA) are you from?
See you later then.

Email introduction

I'm a student at ….
I'm really into ….
What about you?
Send a photo if you've got one.
Bye for now.

Unit 2

Quantity

only one   loads (of)   one or two   a lot of   no

Travel

I want to visit ….
How far is it from here?
It's about fifty minutes from here.
How much is a single / return ticket?

Describing a town / city

It's a town / city.
It's in the north / south / west / east of ….
It's got a population of about ….
My favourite places are ….
It's about … kilometres from ….

Unit 3

Guessing answers

I think it's ….   Maybe / Perhaps it's….
I'm not sure.   I'm sure it's ….
I don't think it's ….

Likes and dislikes

I really enjoy …ing ….   Do you like …ing ….
I hate …ing.   What about you?
(Jake) likes …ing ….   I don't mind …ing ….
What do you like doing?

Country factfile

It has got a border with the (USA) in the (south).
The (Atlantic) is to the east of (Canada).
Most (Canadians) speak (English), but. ….
(French) is the main language in ….
A lot of people from other countries live and work
   there.
In particular, there are a lot of people from ….

Unit 4

Speculating about things you see and hear

It looks like a / an ….
It doesn't look like a / an ….
It sounds like a / an ….
It doesn't sound like a / an ….
Maybe it's a / an ….
I'm sure it's a / an ….

Chatting on the phone

Are you having a good time?
Give me a call.
It's (Jake).
We can meet later if you want.
What are you doing at the moment?
How are you?

Describing wildlife

Females have (one baby), called a (calf), every ….
(Orcas) live in ….
Here they are ….
(Orcas) are on the red list because ….
The animals in this photo are ….

Unit 5

Time expressions

once a day   today
every Tuesday   twice a month
this afternoon   on Friday morning(s)
three times a week   at 5 o'clock
in the afternoon

Requesting, giving and refusing permission

Is it OK if I … ?   Can I / we … ?
No, sorry, you can't.   Yes, you can.
Why not?

Invitations

Do you want to go (into town after school)?
Are you busy (on Saturday)?
That's a pity.
Sounds good.
What about (Saturday) then?
No, sorry, (Jake), I can't.

Giving information

Here's some information about … .
School starts at (8.15) and there are (six) lessons.
The classes are (45 minutes) long.
All students study (English, maths and science).
We can choose … .
There are clubs after school.
You can buy (snack food).

Unit 6

Talking about jobs

I want to be a / an … .
He / She is a / an … .
I think being a / an … is … .
It's a / an … job.
A / An … works in a / an hospital / garage / café /
office / school / theatre.

Past time expressions

last week / month / year / weekend / Saturday
two days / three weeks / 500 years ago
in the 18th century
in 1961 / March 1493
yesterday

Last weekend

How was your weekend?
Were you on your own?
What was (London) like?
Was your weekend good?

Responses

Great thanks.   It was cool.
No. I was with (my cousin).   Yeah, it was brilliant.

City history

… is a city in the (north) of … .
Today the population is … .
It's on … .
It's near … .
In the … century … .
The people of … are called … .
People first lived in … .
Famous (people) from … include … .

Unit 7

Comparing answers

I think the answer is (b).
I'm not sure. Maybe it's (c).
Yes, I agree.
I don't think so. I think the answer is (a).
Yes, you're right.
I don't agree.

Asking about the weekend

Questions

Did you have a good weekend?
What about you?
What did you do?
How was it?
Was it good?

Responses

It was brilliant.   Yeah. Fantastic!
It was OK.   It was terrible. / Not really.
It was boring.

Sports biography

His / Her full name is … .
He / She turned professional when … .
He / She won … in … .
He's / She's got … hair and … eyes.
He / She was born on … .
He / She first … when he / she was three years old.
He / She also won … .

Unit 8

Making and responding to suggestions

Why don't we (find a taxi)?
I'm not sure about that.
How about (getting the bus)?
We can't do that.
Let's (ask someone).
That's a good idea!

Writing a blog

Here I am in my … .
We're going to stay … .
We had a … time.
I'm going to go on an … next … .
This is me in my … .

Infinitive	Past simple	Past participle
be /biː, bɪ/	was /wɒz, wəz/, were /wɜː(r), wə(r)/	been /biːn/
become /bɪˈkʌm/	became /bɪˈkeɪm/	become /bɪˈkʌm/
begin /bɪˈgɪn/	began /bɪˈgæn/	begun /bɪˈgʌn/
break /breɪk/	broke /brəʊk/	broken /ˈbrəʊkən/
build /bɪld/	built /bɪlt/	built /bɪlt/
buy /baɪ/	bought /bɔːt/	bought /bɔːt/
can /kæn/	could /kʊd/	could /kʊd/
catch /kætʃ/	caught /kɔːt/	caught /kɔːt/
come /kʌm/	came /keɪm/	come /kʌm/
do /duː/	did /dɪd/	done /dʌn/
drink /drɪŋk/	drank /dræŋk/	drunk /drʌŋk/
eat /iːt/	ate /eɪt/	eaten /iːtn/
find /faɪnd/	found /faʊnd/	found /faʊnd/
fly /flaɪ/	flew /fluː/	flown /fləʊn/
get /get/	got /gɒt/	got /gɒt/
get up /ˈget ʌp/	got up /ˈgɒt ʌp/	got up /ˈgɒt ʌp/
give /gɪv/	gave /geɪv/	given /gɪvn/
go /gəʊ/	went /went/	gone /gɒn/
have /hæv/	had /hæd/	had /hæd/
hide /haɪd/	hid /hɪd/	hidden /hɪdn/
know /nəʊ/	knew /njuː/	known /nəʊn/
learn /lɜːn/	learnt / learned /lɜːnt/	learnt / learned /lɜːnt/
leave /liːv/	left /left/	left /left/
lose /luːz/	lost /lɒst/	lost /lɒst/
make /meɪk/	made /meɪd/	made /meɪd/
meet /miːt/	met /met/	met /met/
read /riːd/	read /red/	read /red/
run /rʌn/	ran /ræn/	run /rʌn/
say /seɪ/	said /sed/	said /sed/
see /siː/	saw /sɔː/	seen /siːn/
send /send/	sent /sent/	sent /sent/
sit /sɪt/	sat /sæt/	sat /sæt/
sleep /sliːp/	slept /slept/	slept /slept/
speak /spiːk/	spoke /spəʊk/	spoken /ˈspəʊkən/
spend /spend/	spent /spent/	spent /spent/
swim /swɪm/	swam /swæm/	swum /swʌm/
take /teɪk/	took /tʊk/	taken /ˈteɪkən/
teach /tiːtʃ/	taught /tɔːt/	taught /tɔːt/
tell /tel/	told /təʊld/	told /təʊld/
think /θɪŋk/	thought /θɔːt/	thought /θɔːt/
wear /weə(r)/	wore /wɔː(r)/	worn /wɔːn/
write /raɪt/	wrote /rəʊt/	written /rɪtn/